# WESTERN NATIONAL
## OMNIBUS COMPANY

Ian Allan
PUBLISHING

## Colin Morris

# Contents

*Front cover:* The first Bristol Lodekkas for Western National arrived in 1954. No 1883 (RTT 962), a Bristol LD6B/ ECW new in 1955, waits to depart St Ives bus station for Penzance in July 1969.
*Martin Llewellyn / Omincolour*

*Back cover, lower:* Bound for Mylor Bridge on route 561, No 1600 (NFJ 600M) a Bristol LH/6L/ECW 43-seater of 1973 passes the Broadmead Hotel in Kimberley Park Road, Falmouth, in July 1976.
*Mike Stephens*

*Back cover, upper:* Pictured in Totnes Market Square in May 1972 with blinds set for Harbertonford, Bristol SUL4A/ECW dual-purpose 33-seater No 1222 (272 KTA) was originally a coach, numbered 422.
*Mike Stephens*

*Title page:* Centre-stage in a pleasant '60s period piece, Bristol LD6G/ECW 60-seater No 1961 (513 BTA) of 1959 has crossed the River Fal bridge and climbed to stop outside the Town Arms pub in Tregony. The vehicle was operating on service 51 from Truro to Porthscatho, on beautiful Gerrans Bay. *Mike Stephens*

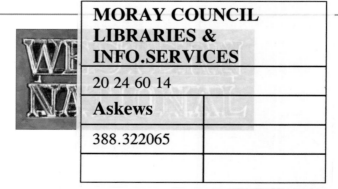

> *For*
> # ANDREW H. WALLER
> *contributor to every one of my transport histories —*
> *and a steadfast friend for longer than either of us cares to disclose*

First published 2008

ISBN (10) 0 7110 3174 6

ISBN (13) 978 0 7110 3174 6

Published by Ian Allan Publishing

an imprint of Ian Allan Publishing Ltd, Hersham, Surrey KT12 4RG

Printed in England by Ian Allan Publishing Ltd, Hersham, Surrey KT12 4RG

Code: 0804/B3

Visit the Ian Allan Publishing website at www.ianallanpublishing.com

# Introduction and Acknowledgements

Thisbook is the second of a pair devoted to outline histories of the two branches of the National Omnibus & Transport Co Ltd set up and operated at differing locations in the South West of England. The first volume, *Southern National Omnibus Company*, was published in 2007. The 'difference' related to the 50% interest in each company acquired by either the Southern Railway or (in the case of the subject of this, the second volume) the Great Western Railway, following the enabling Railway Acts of 1928.

Both Southern National's and Western National's allotted territories were allocated on the basis of geographical similarity to the areas in the West Country served respectively by the Southern and Great Western railway companies, primarily so that each could set up or maintain efficient road/rail connections with its related partner.

The Great Western Railway always considered itself a cut above the rest, doing many things differently from the others — a habit that was to survive post-World War 2 nationalisation, when it became British Railways' Western Region, and continue beyond the eventual phasing-out of steam traction. A proportion of its large passenger-carrying Road Motor Department, however, was pooled in 1929 with a NO&T's West of England operations. Nevertheless, the GWR's representatives upon the resultant Western National's board of directors continued to support their railway company's interests with all the panache and vigour one would associate with its superior 'house style'.

The Western National company's territory was spread across the West Country along the following (railway) lines: south Cornwall and south Devon, followed at a later date by north Somerset, the Stroud area of Gloucestershire and the Trowbridge area of west Wiltshire. The last two areas in particular had been under threat from the growing Bristol Tramways & Carriage Co Ltd since the outset of NO&T's foray into the West of England. However, an extraordinary turn of events, brought about by none other than the Great Western Railway, was to prolong Western National's hold upon its two beleaguered outposts.

Well blessed with West Country cousins, my childhood visits to those parts understandably increased during World War 2. Thus my intro-duction to the affairs of Western National occurred at 8.45 one morning in March 1941, when four red open-staircase double-deck buses roared westward through Crewkerne. "Whoay!" cried an elderly Man o'Zummerzet beside me. "They be Lunnon buzzes, bain't they? What they'm doin' down yer then?" It was many years later that I learned instead that what we had seen were 52-seat Tilling-bodied AEC Regents (Nos 6229/33/62/88) of Brighton, Hove & District scurrying to Plymouth — the advance guard of a relief effort following a devastating attack by the Luftwaffe upon Western National's garage in that proud city. WNOC's own buses — be-laddered saloons in two-tone green — first came to my notice somewhat later, in Chard.

This volume is based largely upon the minutes of Western National's board meetings, which documents are now held by the Kithead Trust in Droitwich and have been made available courtesy of Peter Jaques, my wise collaborator of many years' standing. I have again to record my thanks to my relatives Mollie Rendell, Delia Barrett and Laura Lock, particularly with reference to the activities of Pennell King, Hutchings & Cornelius and Safeway Services. Similarly, help has been given over the years by Harry Rollings, Douglas Morison, Peter Hunt, J. T. Wilson, Eric Jones, Royston Morgan and Michael Rourke, Traffic Manager of WNOC and Managing Director of a later Southern National.

Robert J. Crawley kindly agreed once again to loan material from his and Frank Simpson's Calton Phoenix collection, taking the trouble to meet me in Exeter, Birmingham and Leyland, Lancashire. In addition, for hospitality which has aided research over many years I am indebted to: Mr & Mrs Roger Howard, of North Hill, Launceston, Mr & Mrs Colin Billington, of Fifield, Mr & Mrs Graham Glenister, of Moor Park, and my long-term friends Andrew Waller and Alan Lambert, both of whom regularly peruse and edit my early drafts. Finally most of the excellent coloured illustrations for this volume were provided with great generosity by Mike Stephens, of Lightwater, Surrey.

*Colin Morris*
Heswall
January 2008

**Note:** Readers wishing to study complete details of rolling stock, services run by acquired operators, routes and premises are directed to *The Years Between, 1909-1969, Vol 1: The National Story* and *Vol 3: The Story of Western and Southern National* (1979 and 1990 respectively) by R. J. Crawley *et al.*

# CHAPTER ONE

# The West Country and the Great Western Railway

O N AN AFTERNOON in the latter part of February 1929, four directors of the National Omnibus & Transport Co Ltd and the three able to attend that day to represent the Great Western Railway gathered in London for the very first meeting of the newly formed Western National Omnibus Co Ltd.

Those readers familiar with the works of Thomas Hardy may detect a smidgen of his style borrowed for the opening line of this opening chapter. 'Twas done deliberately to draw attention to an additional attraction superimposed upon the already varied topographical niceties long extant in the verdant South Western peninsula — one which has further increased the number of visitors who come additionally to celebrate West Country worthies both real and fictional.

In particular, the publication of novels by three very different authors spanned the Victorian era, each stepping back in time either to cover the chosen historical period or to avoid the suddenly increased pace of life which marked the progress of the 19th century. Kingsley (1855) upon Elizabethan Devon, Blackmore (1869) upon Exmoor and the later Hardy, oft-times upon a largely re-cast Dorset and greater Wessex, caused an excited response from a readership anxious to engage in 'literary tourism'. What a boon for the suitably located jobmasters. Well before the arrival of the internal combustion engine, providers of coaches and carriages enjoyed a marked increase in traffic.

In celebration of Charles Kingsley's famous work (said to have been written at his father's rectory in Clovelly) an eponymous Westward Ho! was set up beside the Pebble Ridge to the north west of Bideford (with mixed fortune), and a Bideford, Westward Ho! & Appledore Railway was operated by the British Electric Traction company (which named one of the three steam locomotives employed *Kingsley*) until the demands of World War 1 forced the line to close.

In R. D. Blackmore's memorable *Lorna Doone* a 'coach and six' literally becomes the vehicle by which the notorious Doones cause the death of the heroine's remaining family — and then abduct her to serve their long-term monetary purpose.

'Who is who?' at any one time — and 'Where is what?' — feature large in Hardy's 'Wessex', particularly in *Tess of the D'Urbervilles* (1891), where the legendary family's coach plays its recurrent and ominous part. Although Hardy seems to have considered Cornwall to have been part of his fictional 'Lower Wessex', it is doubtful whether any Cornishman would agree that the duchy was ever included in the kingdom. Cornish, a language in the Cymric division of Celtic, was last pronounced with any degree of audible certainty by Dolly Pentreath of Mousehole in the late 18th century. With considerable diplomacy and good business sense, the London promoters of the West Penwith Motor Co Ltd named a 20-seat Milnes-Daimler bus after her in 1903, when it replaced a long-established horse-bus service in the extreme south west of Cornwall (Penwith being the Cornish name for that area). By October of that year, however, the Great Western Railway had 'captured' the locality and provided its own bus routes in extension of its celebrated railway line from Paddington to Penzance — of which more anon.

The directors of the GWR company, formed initially to promote and fund Isambard Kingdom Brunel's *magnum opus*, the construction of a broad-gauge railway line from London to Bristol, had opted to give it an elitist send-off by calling it 'Great'. Practically everyone associated with it thereafter did their utmost to ensure that the 'Great' Western Railway remained just so. Even those companies associated with the GWR were encouraged to cut 30ft swathes through the countryside to accommodate twin tracks each marginally over 7ft wide. In such form the Bristol & Exeter Railway came in sight of the English Channel by 1844.

Literary tourism in action c1960: Bedford OB, LTT 690, of Sherrin's, Carhampton, fords the Badgworthy Water (locally 'Badgery-water') at Malmsmead, beside 'Lorna Doone's Farm'. The notion that this celebrated fictional young lady actually owned a farm calls for even greater imagination than does 'King Arthur's Café' at Tintagel. *F. Frith & Co Ltd / Colin Morris collection*

The first Locomotive Superintendent of the GWR, the youthful Daniel Gooch, was appointed by Brunel in 1837. It was he who took Brunel to fields beside a canal near Swindon and said something like 'This place will do!'. And here was built the famous Swindon Works, birthplace later of GWR's Brunswick-green locomotives and milk-chocolate-and-cream carriages.

Obliged eventually to acknowledge the need to conform with the narrower gauge of 4ft 8½in adopted by neighbouring companies, the GWR itself began to lay such standard-gauge tracks in 1854, but the last broad-gauge lines were not replaced until 1892. Its earlier use nevertheless lent a very spacious air to the works and its environs thereafter.

Meanwhile, at the close of the 19th century, the development of a viable internal-combustion engine made small public-service motor vehicles a distinct possibility. In contrast to the one seven-seat wagonette running in the area at Torquay in 1899, Plymouth — as befitted its size — attracted the setting up in 1900 of the privately owned Plymouth Motor Car Co, in which W. Turner Smith played a leading part. It ran five Coventry-built Daimler wagonettes of similar size between Derry's Clock Tower and Salisbury Road, some 150 yards to the north of Beaumont Road. Sadly for this pioneer of local motor transport, Plymouth Corporation extended its electric tramway along Beaumont Road in 1902, with cars capable of carrying up to eight times as many passengers apiece. In April 1904 W. Turner Smith was looking for another job — and was appointed Traffic Manager of Eastbourne Corporation Motor Omnibus Service. Fifteen months later he became Development Manager for the Motor Omnibus Construction Co

Ltd, at Walthamstow, the first MOC bus emerging in July 1906. Clearly the Plymouth area had lost a talented man.

Thus Plymouth Corporation had commenced its comparatively long and strong defensive stance toward 'outside' operators, but, although it obtained powers to run its own motor omnibuses in 1915, it would not do so until the summer of 1920.

In the very early 20th century the GWR had provided horse buses between its large termini and not-too-distant hotels. Its motor buses were set to be introduced and put to use otherwise. Pressed to construct various railway branch lines radiating from those already established, particularly in the West Country, the GWR opted instead to provide services run by petrol-engined motor buses. Other railway companies were to do likewise, but on

Royal Hotel and Clock Tower, Plymouth

Although Devon was the county that bemoaned more hills of 1 in 5 or worse, the most challenging roads in the West Country were actually to be found in Somerset, on the route between Lynmouth and Minehead — so much so that horses bore the brunt until motor buses could cope. Here Tom Jones's 'Lorna Doone' coach-and-six labours up Countisbury Hill in 1907. Jones also owned the hotel (top left). *Colin Morris collection*

The reverse of the card *(above)*, written to his solicitor by Tom Jones himself on 24 October 1908 and bearing his signature. The 'Lorna Doone' coach was built in Lynton by Reuben Elliott in the late 19th century. Remarkably it survives, restored to its original livery of black and yellow with red wheels, and resides in Devon in the care of Mark Broadbent's 'Phoenix Carriages', whence it may be hired. *Colin Morris collection*

nothing like the scale achieved by GWR. Although most of the early chassis purchased for that purpose were built, together with their bodywork, by Milnes-Daimler in Shropshire, later examples were constructed by such coachwork firms as Bayleys, Birch Bros and Dodson.

From 1905 some bodywork was built and fitted by the GWR itself at its Road Vehicle Shop, set up beside the disused and in-filled North Wilts Canal, by now located in the midst of the vastly expanded Swindon Works. Based there and placed in charge of the newly established Great Western Road Motor Department was Fulwar Cecil Ashton Coventry, destined to play an important part in the fortunes of the future Western National Omnibus Co Ltd — until his death in office in 1944. Forty years earlier, however, he supervised the construction and fitting of that in-house GWR bodywork. Among the more impressive examples was an early (1905) observation car with open sides, which utilised spare Milnes parts such as its ornate bracing brackets (see illustration; it was, incidentally, not a charabanc, having but one entrance door on each side and a central gangway). If this was constructed at the same time as the chassis, it pipped by some 12 months Douglas Mackenzie's innovative slipper design for the Clacton-on-Sea Omnibus Co and the Sussex Motor Road Car Co — but must have

been equally unstable when driven fully loaded around a corner.

The launch on 17 August 1903 of what the GWR claimed as 'the first railway motor-omnibus service' — that between Helston and The Lizard (the most southerly location in mainland Britain) — is described in the companion *Southern National Omnibus Company* volume (2007), as both Milnes-Daimler vehicles involved had previously done similar duty in conjunction with the Lynton & Barnstaple Railway. Nevertheless, those Great Western Road Motor services which were eventually to contribute a major part in the foundation of the Western National Omnibus Co Ltd are outlined in this chapter. For a full description of them — and of other GWR bus services in England beyond the West Country and in Wales — readers are directed to Cummings (1980).

As described in *Glory Days: Devon General* (2006), Devon has by far the greatest number of roads with a maximum gradient of 1 in 5 (or worse) of any British county. Not surprising, then, that the Great Western Railway's innovative bus services did much of their work in Cornwall, the flatter fringes of south Devon and points east of that county (which is where the unbuilt branch railway lines would have gone anyway). Thus, for the first two decades of the 20th century, steeper contours of the West Country remained the preserve of the coach-and-four, plus at least two additional horses (with mounted postilion) to help out.

Yet, even in terrain such as this, if the GWR had a railway line it felt needed support, it took an interest in equine road transport. One such was the perceived need to curtail the influence of the rival London & South Western Railway upon the Lynton/Lynmouth area, by extending its own presence westward from its rail terminus at Minehead, in north Somerset. The physical snag here was that the steepest hill in the West Country, 'winding badly and very rough', was at Porlock, halfway between Minehead and County Gate ('Cosgate'), the border with Devon. And the added attraction of the latter was that it was (and remains) very much part of R. D. Blackmore's 'Doone country'. Even before it had invested in its own motor-bus services the GWR had subsidised the operation of the celebrated 'Lorna Doone' coach-and-six, run from the Royal Castle Hotel, Lynton, to Minehead (and return) by turn-of-the-century proprietor Thomas Baker.

Both hotel and coach were bought from Baker by Tom Jones (a real one, not the fictional picaresque by Henry Fielding — which probably influenced both Blackmore and Hardy). He continued to run the 'Lorna Doone' where motor buses feared to go, together with others, including Harold Langdon, who ran also the 'Red Deer' horse-drawn

All friends together. Also *en route* to Minehead, although not really in competition with the 'Lorna Doone' coach, Harold Langdon's 'Red Deer' coach-and-six has come to its customary halt beside the Ship Inn, Porlock, courtesy of a newly constructed easier section of road, for the use of which a toll was charged. The sender of the card had just completed a five-hour trudge to the Rest and Be Thankful Hotel at Wheddon Cross, in the middle of Exmoor. *Colin Morris collection*

coach between the same points, save that he paid a toll to use a new private section that was less steep and went past the Ship Hotel at Porlock. That the Lynmouth–Minehead route could be safely tackled by a motor bus was possibly first proven in June 1913 by Douglas Mackenzie and Alfred Cannon's Daimler CC of Sussex Tourist Coaches; to paraphrase Macaulay (as did one of the passengers in a contemporary account of this exploit):

> '… *the tale's repeated still*
> *How the big Worthing motor drove*
> *Up Countisbury Hill.*'

Both Tom Jones of Lynton and James Hardy of Minehead motorised the route on a regular basis

from the 1920 season. (For a full record of these events see Crawley *et al*, 1979 and 1990.)

Meanwhile, having established itself as a bus operator at Helston and Penzance, the GWR in 1904 began running bank-holiday circular tours from Falmouth to Mullion Cove to The Lizard. In that year also a service of double-deck GWR buses was running along the bight of Mounts Bay between Newlyn and Marazion, the stopping-off place for a low-tide walk to St Michael's Mount and a look at the brass imprint of Queen Victoria's first footfall upon the top landing step.

From such beginnings the GWR established a good coverage of services in western Cornwall, extending from Land's End to a line stretching

For the first two decades of the motor-bus era body-swaps were commonplace among the larger operators. However, upon its launch, at least, No 6 (AF 65), a 20hp Milnes-Daimler, seems to have been the first double-deck motor bus in the West Country. It was attracting a great deal of attention outside Penzance railway station on 10 March 1904, on which date it inaugurated the Newlyn–Marazion service. *Ian Allan Library*

Milnes-Daimler No 9 (A 5014) was said to be capable of carrying 22 passengers (although that, of course, depended upon whether or not its amidships luggage/mail compartment was fully occupied in its intended role). A 20hp model purchased in August 1905, it was put to work on the GWR's original motor-bus route between Helston station and The Lizard. *Alan Lambert collection*

across the neck of the duchy from Porthtowan in the north to Falmouth on the south coast. Farther east a separate web of routes, centred upon St Austell, reached both north and south shorelines, eventually serving widely spaced Porthscatho, Truro and Bodmin at its extremities — and in June 1904 the GWR based a bus at both Callington and Saltash to meet the ferry across the River Tamar to Plymouth. That summer, what was to become the Great Western Railway's famous non-stop 'Cornish Riviera Express' was introduced, further boosting the popularity of western Cornwall.

'Back in England', as the Cornish would have it, the GWR reinforced its provision of road-rail interchange in May 1904 by running services

from Brixham Road station, on the Plymouth–Yealmpton branch line, to Modbury, where strong opposition was encountered from vehicles of similar size run by South Hams Carriers Ltd — both displacing a service of horse buses in the process. Each entered Plymouth itself that year, their buses considerably bigger than the recently departed wagonettes of Turner Smith's Plymouth Motor Co.

In July 1904 the GWR Road Motor Department set up shop at Paignton upon another 'Riviera', that of Torbay (see *Glory Days: Devon General*) thus, in the long term, giving the future Western National Omnibus Co the excuse to claim in a not-too-serious dispute with Devon General: 'Well, we were here first!' That, together with a base established at

In the early days of motor-bus operation (and not surprisingly) the GWR despatched its vehicles to their respective operating areas by rail. Here, at a special loading-gauge platform, Milnes-Daimler No 18 (AF 86) is secured to a dedicated low-loading truck prior to its journey to the West Country. Bridges along the way meant that the roof-mounted luggage rack would be fitted upon arrival. *Alan Lambert collection*

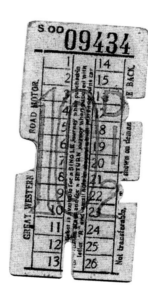

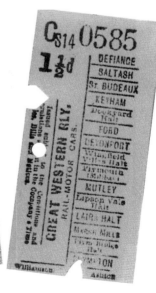

*Above:* Tourism, and literary tourism in particular, was bound to be a winner in the West Country, and when the motor bus began to oust the jobmaster's horse and carriage the GWR was quick to seize the initiative. Local tours began early; from 1904 Milnes-Daimler No 19 (A 6048), a 20hp model capable of carrying 33 passengers, was based at Falmouth station for just such a purpose.
*Alan Lambert collection*

Kingsbridge, enabled the GWR to set up a string of motor-bus services which, in the main, skirted the coastal edges of Dartmoor Forest from Yelverton in the west around to Widecombe-in-the-Moor, reached from Newton Abbot in the east.

As described in the Southern National volume, the London & South Western Railway's pair of Milnes-Daimlers beat the GWR's into Chagford by a short head in 1906 — and the latter's run to and from Moretonhampstead was a far less taxing journey than LSWR's from Exeter! However, tours were not being neglected by the GWR at this time, and at one stage there was an unusual one into Cornwall from Plymouth that crossed the Tamar on the Torpoint Ferry. Such touring facilities were advertised nationwide by GWR buses going as far as Inverness, covered in appropriate advertisements.

By 1910 Dartmoor had become a favourite part of a circular tour — and 'literary tourism' was by no means forgotten. In time honoured fashion, the 'suck it and see' approach to route extensions in the West Country was a feature of the pre-World War 1 development of stage-carriage services. It was, however, World War War 1 which, in its aftermath, was to provide a larger and more reliable chassis-and-engine combination, which was to give bus operators a much greater carrying capacity and a degree of certainty. These were also the first GWR

buses to go out on service fitted with electric lights, rather than the then more familiar oil or acetylene sort. In the GWR's case it was the ex-Army 45hp AEC Y type which provided just what was needed. No fewer than 117 refurbished examples entered the GWR Road Motor fleet throughout its several areas between 1919 and 1924, of which just one, No 279 (LU 9589), a 31-seat GWR-built saloon, survived long enough to join the Western National fleet in 1929. Many of the others would at that time be retained by the GWR for use as lorries. There was plenty of life left in these old dogs of war.

Cummings (1980) records that by 1919 there were GWR Road Motor depots at Penzance, Helston, Redruth, St Austell, Saltash, Modbury, Kingsbridge, Paignton and Chagford. Bridgwater, Stroud and Westbury (with a route extending northward to Trowbridge) were also centres to benefit from a GWR Road Motor presence. With the department already in possession of 10 'Burford' half-cab saloons, a couple of which worked on the original Helston–Lizard route in 1924, 25 Burfords with full-fronted bodywork were added to the fleet, several of which were allocated to the West Country, and 13 examples with pneumatic tyres, both saloons and charabancs, found their way into the Western National fleet in 1929. Two small-capacity Chevrolet charabancs,

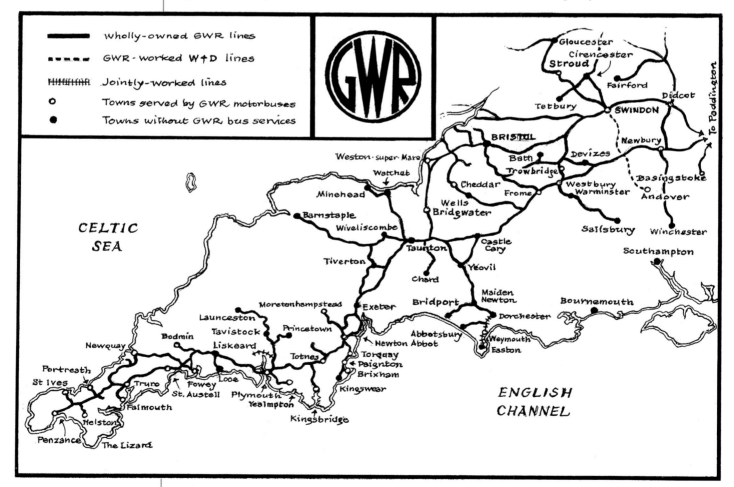

*Above:* Afield near Chagford on a pre-season private-hire trip in 1910 is Cornish-registered GWR 20hp Milnes-Daimler No 45 (AF 86). This vehicle, weighing some $3\frac{1}{2}$ tons, was fitted with a 24-seat, GWR-built open-sided observation-car body, braced by the ornate bracket-work of the period. The driver — a role greatly admired in those days — looks very much in command. The brakes have been firmly applied, and a back-up chock has been placed in front of the nearside rear wheel. The trippers are in good hands. *Kithead Trust / Colin Morris*

*Above:* Simmering nicely at the terminus of the Paignton & Dartmouth Railway in 2005 is GWR '45xx' 2-6-2 tank No 4555. Built at Swindon Works to a 1906 design by Locomotive Superintendent G. J. Churchward, this 57-ton locomotive — with copper and brass fittings giving that extra GWR sparkle — epitomises the justifiable 'swank' of most things Great Western. What a contrast, however, with the Milnes-Daimler's flimsy-looking observation-car body (pictured above), designed at the same works just one year previously by F. C. A. Coventry. *Colin Morris*

In 1905 the GWR took delivery of three 12hp, 12-seat Maudslays with bodywork by the Gloucester Railway Carriage & Wagon Co Ltd, the first being exhibited at that year's Commercial Motor Show. Of the three, one worked in South Wales, one was based at Slough, and the other was rumoured to have been sent to the West Country, although precisely where is unknown.
*Ian Allan Library*

The GWR's first large-capacity vehicles — and the first equipped with electric lighting — were refurbished ex-Army lorry chassis purchased from the Associated Equipment Company (AEC) in 1919. Although registered in Buckinghamshire, No 232 (BH 0274) was, like most of its fellows, not restricted to use solely in its county of origin, and many such 'foreigners' worked in the West Country.
*Ian Allan Library*

In the mid-1920s the products of H. G. Burford & Co Ltd attracted the attention of F. C. A. Coventry, the GWR's Road Motor Superintendent. No fewer than 20 Burford D models joined the fleet in 1924, to be followed by 40 full-fronted ND models in 1925; all were 18seaters. No 859 (XY 7431) was one of a number bodied by the GWR at Swindon Works. It would retain its fleet number upon joining Western National in 1929. *Ian Allan Library*

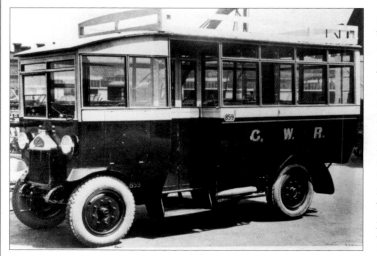

Nos 353/6 (XU 2160/3), bought in 1924 as chasers of competitors' buses, survived to join them.

Thornycroft was favoured with a very large order from the GWR in 1925 — 41 examples of that firm's 19-seat A1 model, all bodied by Vickers. Fourteen of those, sent to the Penzance and Kingsbridge depots, were set to join WNOC. From 1926 the Maudslay ML3, with 32-seat bodywork by Buckingham, Hall Lewis, Strachan & Brown and Vickers, saw service in the West Country, 47 eventually joining WNOC; also the less spritely Guy FBB with the same seating capacity, 22 of which did likewise, as did three further Thornycroft A1s with GWR-built 18-seat bodywork, new in 1928. In addition a mixed collection of vehicles, several acquired from absorbed operators' fleets, were also earmarked for the WNOC. This comprised examples, both saloons and charabancs, manufactured by ADC, Albion, Lancia, Leyland, Morris, Overland and SPA, the last-named marque being imported to Britain by Fiat (England) Ltd. Most of these came from Ashcroft of Paignton, recently bought by the GWR, but were handed over, before entry into its service, direct to Western National in January 1929 (see *Glory Days: Devon General*).

*Left:* Aside from a single J type acquired second-hand for use in Wales the GWR had not purchased Thornycroft products for use as motor buses. A gratefully received boost for the Basingstoke firm's workforce came late in 1924 with an order for no fewer than 40 A1 chassis, to be fitted with 19-seat bodywork by Vickers. No 914 (XY 5375) was licensed in May 1925. Fourteen of its fellows would join WNOC in 1929. *Alan Lambert collection*

*Right:* Purchased in August 1924, initially for private-hire and excursion work in the Slough area, were ten 22hp Chevrolet 14-seaters, some of them fitted with Vickers charabanc bodywork. Two found their way into the Western National fleet in 1929; like fellow-survivor No 353, No 356 (XU 2163) would retain its fleet number thereafter. *Alan Lambert collection*

*Below:* It was not unusual in the 1920s for a manufacturer to seek the permission of an operator to exhibit a prototype vehicle in its colours. If such were the case with this example, or whether it was simply a tempter toward the purchase of further A1 Long chassis, is unknown, but this particular Thornycroft A1 Long (chassis No 12378) was not bought by the GWR. *Colin Morris collection*

To the foregoing must be added the main body of vehicles ordered by the GWR but which instead were delivered (in chocolate-and-cream livery) direct to WNOC in 1929, bearing the fleetname 'Western National'. In this category were three more Burfords, two more Thornycroft A1s, a dozen uprated Thornycroft A2 / Duple 20-seat saloons (see Chapter 3) and 18 further Maudslay ML3B variations of the standard 32-seat saloon, bodied by Buckingham and Vickers.

Thus the Great Western Railway's contribution to the newly formed Western National Omnibus Co's fleet was (along with much else in garages, booking offices and other property, road/rail interchange arrangements and knowledgeable personnel) a total of 96 single-deck omnibuses, which, together with support vans, lorries and a handful of taxis, came to a total of just over 100 vehicles deemed fit for further use. Whisper it softly, however, that the total number of vehicles acquired the previous year (1928) for the already mooted 'Western National' from the Devon Motor Transport / Cornwall Motor Transport fleets was … 148!

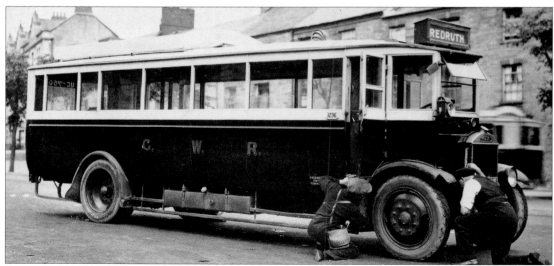

*Left:* No 1278 (YF 5746) was one of a batch of 1927 Guy FBB saloons delivered to the GWR, 22 of them bodied by Vickers as 32-seaters. Just four of this combination (Nos 1265/8/73/9) would pass to Western National in 1929. A drawing of this type had graced the cover of the GWR's bus timetables. *Alan Lambert collection*

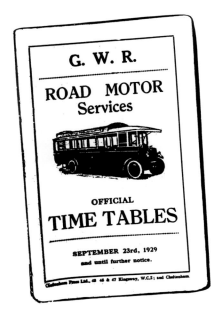

*Above:* A 1927 Guy FBB/Vickers 32-seat saloon adorns the front of the GWR's Road Motor Services timetable effective 23 September 1929 onwards. Although much of its bus fleet had by now been absorbed into geographically appropriate bus companies, there remained in some areas technicalities requiring the railway to act *pro tem* on their behalf. *Kithead Trust*

*Right:* The GWR having taken a financial interest (up to a third or a half) in various existing territorial bus companies, 1929 became a year in which saloon buses in chocolate and cream were frequently to be seen buzzing along, on trade plates to their new homes. This 1928 Thornycroft A1 with GWR 18-seat bodywork was 'snapped' *en route* to the Thames Valley Traction Co Ltd. *Alan Lambert collection*

*Above:* One of four Gilford 166OT/Wycombe 22-seat coaches (the usual chassis/body combination for this type) bought by the GWR in 1929 for its 'express coach service' linking Cheltenham and Oxford stations. With their six-cylinder Lycoming engines and luxurious interiors they were well suited to the task. In 1932 all four passed to the Bristol Tramways & Carriage Co Ltd, by then a Western National subsidiary. *Alan Lambert collection*

# National in the South West of England

In 1904 the GWR purchased three 18-seater Clarkson 20hp steam buses. Road Motor Department No 36 (DA 81) and its fellows were tried out in several places in a search for local water that would suit their boilers; between April and December 1905 all three tried their best from a base in Cheddar on a service to Highbridge and Burnham-on-Sea. *Ian Allan Library*

**M**ENTION is made (and an illustration provided) in the companion Southern National volume of the first large self-propelled road motor vehicle on a stage-carriage service in the West of England. This was the steam-powered LIFU road train which ran between Cirencester and Fairford between 1897 and 1899, the Great Western Railway having demonstrated an early interest in such activity by joining forces with the Midland & South Western Junction Railway to help launch the enterprise.

In the event, the road train proved altogether too cumbersome, and — as described in Chapter 1 — the Great Western Railway turned (almost) exclusively to petrol-powered road vehicles when

launching its Road Motor services from 1903 onward. The single exception to that choice came in September of the following year, when three Clarkson 20hp steam buses were registered to be employed on service between Wolverhampton and Bridgnorth. There they proved unsatisfactory, and they were transferred to Cheddar (Somerset) for use between that base and Burnham-on-Sea from April to September 1905. They were moved to Buckinghamshire at one stage and then given a final chance based upon Bridgwater (Somerset again) in 1906. An appropriate volume of mineral salts in the water was necessary for the continuing good health of earlier Clarkson boilers, and it seems that, away from Torquay (see *Glory Days: Devon General*), such water was difficult to find. The GWR sold its Clarksons in 1907. Nevertheless, their designer, Thomas Clarkson, based at Chelmsford, Essex, persevered with the refinement and construction of his paraffin- and steam-powered vehicles and earned himself a place in the history of the British motor-bus industry, not least because there grew from his determined efforts to perfect and operate profitable omnibus services run solely by steam-powered vehicles an organisation (taken from his hands, eventually) which became the National Omnibus & Transport Co Ltd — forerunner of the Eastern National, Southern National and Western National companies.

Clarkson's steam buses sold nationwide and throughout the British Empire — none more spectacular than the quartet bought by the London & South Western Railway (see *Southern National Omnibus Company*, 2007) for service between Exeter and Chagford at one stage in their careers. But wherever Clarkson steamers were purchased it was but in penny numbers. Thomas Clarkson's hopes were raised considerably by the trial batches bought by the London General Omnibus Co Ltd and the London Road Car Co, both on the threshold of opting for some form of motor transport. Such expectation was duly dashed, however, when both important metropolitan

Thomas Clarkson's 'Chelmsford' single-deck steam-powered buses served at numerous locations in the British Isles, frequently on a trial basis. A common problem was a lack of compatibility 'twixt the boiler and the local water supply. Chelmsford-registered F 1247 is pictured at Headcorn, Kent, where it had attracted a one-man band, a rather nice dog and boys young and old. *Alan Lambert collection*

The National Steam Car Co's London-based fleet comprised more than 200 double-deckers bodied by Hurst Nelson and seating 34 passengers apiece. The chassis were built at the company's Moulsham Works in Chelmsford, in which town they were registered. No 65 (F 5267) of 1912 is accompanied by a conductor and two fitters inside the Nunhead Lane premises in Peckham. The vehicle is fitted with lightweight steel road wheels designed by William Morison.
*Alan Lambert collection*

operators opted instead to purchase buses with petrol-fired internal combustion engines. Gathering influential friends and monetary support around him, Clarkson took the bold step of launching his own bus operation in London. Following the timely transportation of some troops in an 'anti-invasion' exercise, Clarkson made the inspired decision to celebrate his contribution to the nation's security by labelling his first production batch of open-top double-deckers 'NATIONAL'. Thus it was the National Steam Car Co which began running upon its first route — Shepherd's Bush to Lambeth North — in November 1909, its vehicles dressed in an outstanding livery of white and gold. Each bus glided along emitting a *sotto voce* hiss which contrasted noticeably with the racket put up by the chattering engines and noisy final drive to the rear wheels of their main rivals, the embryonic petrol-engined vehicles of the LGOC and LRCC.

National's buses in London became very popular, especially with the ladies — always a good sign. Reconstituted as the National Steam Car Co (1911) Ltd, the company extended its routes as far afield as Stoke Newington, Hampton Court, Dulwich and Bexley. When in World War 1 the LGOC's efficient and famous B-type double-deckers were commandeered in large numbers for service with the forces fighting in France, Clarkson's steamers stepped into the gap created in the metropolitan network, and during that period their numbers expanded to just short of the 200 mark.

From July 1913, having bought the Chelmsford-based bus services of the Great Eastern Railway, the NSCC ran to some nine destinations in Essex. From that humble beginning stemmed Western National's associated company, the Eastern National Omnibus Co Ltd. (See *Glory Days: Eastern National*.)

The brake upon the expansion of the LGOC imposed by military requirements in World War 1 was disengaged following the Allied victory in 1918. Within a year the resurgent LGOC had entered into a territorial agreement with National, whereby the former would relinquish its services in Bedfordshire in exchange for an arrangement under which the latter withdrew (almost) completely from its former haunts in London proper. The exception was that National should retain its Shepherd's Bush depot for the sole purpose of its private-hire and tours work within and from the capital to points beyond.

Thus National was obliged to take to the provinces in a search for new territory in which to operate. In addition to expanding its operations based upon Chelmsford and Bedford it elected to 'go west'. The first foothold was made somewhat to the north east of what became the company's stronghold in England's south-western peninsula — at Stroud, Gloucestershire. Credit for that goes to the financiers Clare & Co and in particular to Lt Col O. C. Clare, who became a director of the National Steam Car Co Ltd (and, later, NO&T). Approached in the summer of 1919 by a two-man business called Gloucestershire Carriers Ltd, his finance house decided to introduce the proprietors to the National company, which took over the proposed new bus service before it got going. In October of that year an initial depot was set up beneath railway arches at Wallbridge, Stroud. The traffic potential was rather sparse, but the locale's well-treed and ravine-like valleys offered

First licensed in May 1907, this double-decker was delivered to the Great Eastern Railway for duty on one of the isolated group of services operated in East Anglia. It was one of three Maudslay 30hp buses, Nos 19-21 (F 2440-2), with 36-seat bodywork by the Gloucester Railway Carriage & Wagon Co Ltd. The GER's Chelmsford-area services were acquired by Thomas Clarkson in July 1913 — and operated thereafter by his steam buses.
*Alan Lambert collection*

a beautiful foretaste of the kind of country the company would encounter later in the depths of Devonshire.

In setting up its series of routes based upon Stroud, National incurred the wrath of the Bristol Tramways & Carriage Co Ltd, which considered it to be invading territory already earmarked as part of Bristol's own back yard. The latter set out to defend that territory. Klapper (1978) recalls looking down as late as 1921 from a Cotswold escarpment near Cheltenham and seeing 'a white National double-decker followed along the same narrow road by a blue single-deck 4-ton Bristol and thinking how stupid of two responsible bus operators to be competing for traffic in such thin territory!'. This was the first area in which National rubbed shoulders with the Bristol company — a relationship the demands of finance would improve considerably a decade later, after the formation of Western National (see Chapter 3). After Stroud the move into the West Country was supervised by Walter James Iden, by now Managing Director jointly with Thomas Clarkson, the latter by now concerned almost exclusively with the development of what he hoped would be further steam chassis for use by the company. Iden, on the other hand, had experience with the Motor Manufacturing Co Ltd (MMC), Crossley, the LGOC, the Tramways (MET) Omnibus Co Ltd and AEC. Very much an advocate of the petrol-engined omnibus, he had joined National in 1918 at the express invitation of its Chairman, a director since 1915, Kenneth Hawksley. If Clarkson saw what was coming, it did not deter him from his chosen path. Asked for his opinion, Iden recommended that the company adopt exclusively the petrol-powered motor bus —

a view which the board accepted. Clarkson resigned; William Morison, his assistant from the earliest days and a co-patent-holder, remained with National as Chief Engineer and spent the rest of his working life with the company and its future subsidiaries. The company duly re-equipped with AEC YC chassis — and a few 3-ton Dennises — and elected to change its name to the National Omnibus & Transport Co Ltd, which it registered on 13 February 1920. W. J. Iden was to shape the destiny of both the future Southern and Western National companies in the West Country, remaining at the helm until 1932, when he, in turn, would be ousted, but by a change in company ownership.

The second National director to have joined the board from Clare & Co in 1918 was John J. Jarvis (not to be confused with John 'Jack' Jarvis of Devon General). Following the premature death of Hawksley in 1922, Jarvis — by now Sir John Jarvis Bt, in recognition of the sterling work he put into the rejuvenation of industry at Jarrow, following crippling unemployment in that town — became Chairman of National. In 1921 Henry G. Burford and Henry C. Merrett had joined the board also. Burford had been an engineer with Milnes-Daimler Ltd and was now the prime mover of H. G. Burford & Co Ltd of North Kensington. His small-capacity Burford saloon buses became popular with the GWR in the early 'Twenties, and nine Hickman-bodied examples were purchased by National. Merrett's expertise lay in the field of accountancy with Merrett, Son & Street of London; he was also a director of the United Counties Omnibus Co Ltd.

National now turned its attention to Bridgwater, Somerset, where it rented premises from the Bridgwater Motor Garage Co and on 21 July 1920 commenced a service through the town from Taunton to Burnham-on-Sea. Bristol Tramways then introduced a service south to Bridgwater — and National responded by going farther north, to Weston super Mare. The company then purchased the business of White Bros & Bates, based upon South Petherton. This gave National its first access to Yeovil and an outstation in South Petherton some seven years before three local firms — Hutchings, Cornelius and Gunn's Safeway Services, all of that village — began operating. In Yeovil National's buses were initially based near Penn Mill station, but in August 1921 the company acquired the Reckleford Works, previously occupied by Petter's Engineering Ltd. A key route was quickly established westward to Crewkerne and thereafter southward to West Bay on the Dorset coast. In relation to the occupation of the ex-Petter's building it is of note that working there with that firm beforehand had been Percy Frost Smith, who joined Thomas Tilling Ltd to take charge of motor-omnibus development. Together with W. A. Stevens he developed the Tilling-Stevens petrol-electric chassis. The firm built around its production eventually faltered in the 'Thirties, and Tilling was to do its unsuccessful best to get Bristol,

Western National and other associated firms to help bail it out. (See Chapter 3.)

In the autumn of 1920 National found a base in Taunton, where it housed some buses in the South Street end of Thomas' Posting Establishment. There was a small tramway in Taunton, and, conveniently for National, its operator, the Taunton Electric Traction Co Ltd, got itself into bad odour with its electricity supplier — the Corporation of Taunton, no less — and was obliged to cease operating. The local council greeted with many thanks National's offer to replace its services with motor buses from August 1921. The company thus

secured the centre of its local operations, which then reached out to Bridgwater, Burnham-on-Sea and on to Weston-super-Mare (more competition for Bristol Tramways), to Yeovil, Rockwell Green and Wiveliscombe. Closing the gap between Taunton and Yeovil completed a barrier to whatever designs the Bristol company might have had in relation to possible territorial gains in the South West peninsula.

Shortage of vehicles prevented National from putting up any opposition to Bristol Tramways' eastward march toward Swindon, Wiltshire, which effectively put a stop to realistic expansion south of Stroud by National. In that quarter National had briefly operated services to the south-west of Stroud (in an area detached from the rest by some four miles) from a base at Wotton-under-Edge with two

roundabout routes, to Charfield and to Uley. This really was very much in Bristol territory, and the latter prevailed. Considerably longer-lived was the base established in August 1921 at Trowbridge, Wiltshire, to which the ex-Wotton-under-Edge personnel and vehicles repaired in the manner of refugees. Having set itself up in an office in the Market Place, National went on to provide services from there to Chippenham (with an extension to Calne), Frome, Devizes, Broughton Gifford, Bradford-on-Avon, Warminster, Bratton and Farleigh Hungerford and succeeded in linking up northward to Stroud via Malmesbury.

More 'thin' territory was tested by establishing an outstation at Wincanton (Somerset), whence services onward to Mere, Shaftesbury and Blandford threatened the territorial plans of both Wilts &

Dorset and Hants & Dorset Motor Services Ltd. In the event, a line linking Mere, Semley, Shaftesbury, Blandford Forum, Wareham and Swanage came to represent the eastern limit of National territory in Wiltshire and Dorset, although the road between Shaftesbury and Blandford itself became a Hants & Dorset preserve.

At this early stage in its West Country career National also contemplated opening a depot at Swindon, which, had it done so, would have provided a more-than-appropriate link with headquarters of its future partner, the Great Western Railway. Baulked by the eastward advance of the Bristol company, National instead drove westward, for some while calling a halt at Exeter, where it came to a territorial agreement with the Devon General Omnibus & Touring Co Ltd — and for just one month National held shares in that company, during which time W. J. Iden was briefly one of its directors. (See *Glory Days: Devon General*.)

After 1921 the white livery inherited from the National Steam Car Co Ltd was abandoned in favour of bottle green. In the days when many of the rural roads to be traversed had yet to be tarmacadamed, this was quickly bespattered with mud. As a short-term measure whilst more washing facilities were set up, many of the AEC YC saloons and charabancs then prevalent in the fleet were sent out on service with only the bonnet and vertical dash in green, the rest of the bodywork being painted pale grey. This disguised dried mud splashes surprisingly well.

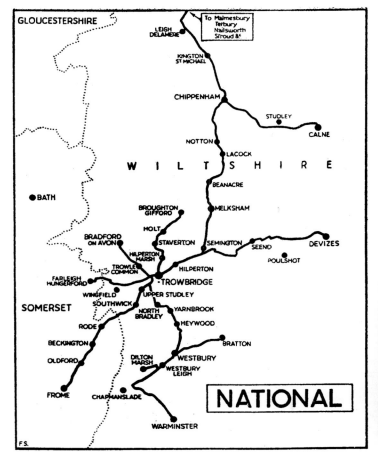

Lighter than the ex-Army AEC Y-type chassis with which National had turned to petrol-engined buses was the ex-LGOC B-type double-decker, of which 45 with standard 34-seat LGOC bodywork joined the National fleet in 1921 as a stopgap measure pending the arrival of new vehicles. Four were cut down as 26-seater saloons. Hired ex-LGOC B5025 (LH 8554) displays the new-style fleetname on a dark-red background.
*The Omnibus Society*

In 1922 National put down a marker along the South Coast between Swanage (Dorset) in the east and Seaton (Devon) in the west. Three separate services were involved, Swanage–Weymouth, Weymouth–Bridport–West Bay and West Bay–Axminster–Seaton. Pictured working the middle section is AEC YC No 2097 (HK 9406), with metal-panelled Dodson bodywork in red-lined grey; 'Upwey' is mis-spelled.
*E. G. P. Masterman*

The early 'Twenties was very much an era of trial and error: extensions and 'fingers outward' from established routes came and went, sometimes because the available buses were sent where routes elsewhere seemed more profitable, particularly seaside ones in summertime on both north and south coasts. In Wiltshire both National and Wilts & District reeled back somewhat as Lavington & Devizes Motor Services joined forces with the Bath Tramways Motor Co. Such opposition curtailed the expansion of services based upon Trowbridge, whilst the Bristol Tramways & Carriage Co Ltd set out determinedly to put the squeeze upon National's services in the Stroud area. In contrast, Bridgwater, Bridport, Taunton, Weymouth and Yeovil became well-established depots which offered good opportunities for the company's expansion. A strengthened position at Weymouth was gained in April 1925 when National acquired Luton-based Road Motors Ltd and its 'interloping' services in that seaside resort. An agreement with Chaplin & Rogers' Chard Motors not to compete on the route to Seaton was made (and observed, after a fashion); the latter firm was destined to become a joint Southern/Western National purchase in 1932.

Whereas Taunton and Bridgwater — plus the beleaguered Stroud and Trowbridge — were firmly in the area destined to become Western National territory, that south of Yeovil was to be allotted to the sister Southern National company. (See Morris 2007.) The big breakthrough to the west of an established north–south route coast-to-coast between Minehead and Exeter was about to be made. Early in 1927 National acquired the Hardy Central Garage Co of Minehead, together comprising James Harvey's 'Silver Streak' tours, Minehead & District Motor Services, and (from Lynton westward)

Hardy-Colwills Motor Service. The last-named provided stage-carriage services centred on several locations westward, all within range of the north Devon/ Cornwall coast as far as Newquay. As practically all of that area was served by the Southern Railway it was destined to pass to Southern National when National's territory in the West Country was disparted in 1929. (See Morris 2007.)

In contrast, the big breakthrough to the west (as far as Penzance), which was to become a very important part of the future Western National network, came at the close of 1927 with National's purchase of the Devon Motor Transport Co Ltd and its (fleetname-only) subsidiary 'Cornwall Motor Transport'. With 85 routes and 140 service buses (mostly Bristol, Albion, Thornycroft and Maudslay, together with five Karriers, two Lancias and one each of Star, Morris, Leyland and Daimler), it was NO&T's biggest acquisition. In contrast with those of Hardy-Colwills, most DMT routes were within sight of the southern coast of Devon, and CMT's a large part of both coasts in Cornwall.

The founder of Devon Motor Transport was an ex-serviceman who built up a transport business with his WW1 gratuity grant, not only succeeding but creating a very large undertaking over a considerable area. Cdr Francis T. Hare RN started with a small fleet of petrol and steam lorries at Okehampton in December 1919 and first ran bus services the following year. Although the head office and repair works remained in Okehampton, area offices were opened in Plymouth and Truro, in addition to garages in both locations; others

This photograph records something of a triumph for Thornycroft's vehicle-manufacturing arm at Basingstoke. Devon Motor Transport No 110 (CO 7875) was the first completed vehicle of a very large batch of A1 models produced for that firm, more than 50 being delivered in 1925/6. When NO&T acquired DMT in 1928 this example became No 2675, surviving thereafter — along with the rest of the batch — to form part of the opening Western National fleet of 1929. *Colin Morris collection*

National Omnibus & Transport Co routes in Devon, Somerset and Dorset prior to the 'march west' in 1927.

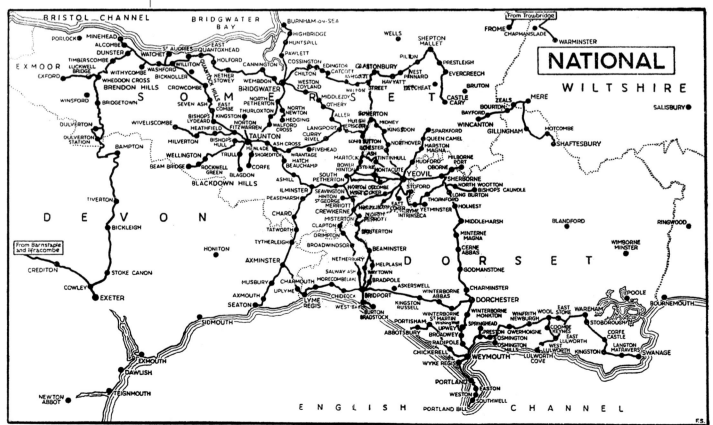

All bar one of the saloon-bus version of the Thornycroft A1 vehicles delivered to DMT were bodied by Vickers, and all but seven of these were 20-seaters, the exceptions being based upon the A1 Long chassis and seating 24 passengers. DMT No 137 (CO 9342) became No 2702 in the NO&T (and, later, Western National) fleet.
*Colin Morris collection*

An odd-man-out amidst the Vickers-bodied Thornycrofts delivered in 1925/6 was DMT No 135 (CO 9074). Based on the long-wheelbase version of the A1 chassis, it was bodied instead by Northern Counties, of Wigan, and could be identified by its deeper roof and waistband, together with a front elevation that lacked a destination box. It became WNOC No 2700.
*Colin Morris collection*

were established at Camborne, Liskeard, Penryn, Perranporth, Penzance, St Austell, Tamerton Foliot and Tavistock, along with numerous outstations elsewhere in both Devon and Cornwall. In order to avoid any local antipathy in Cornwall toward vehicles marked 'DMT', most of the buses running in the duchy bore the CMT (Cornwall Motor Transport) title — after DMT had acquired the assets and licences of the Cornwall Enterprise Motors Ltd of Perranporth — but, curiously, the timetable booklets made no such distinction. At one stage DMT was the parent company of the Jersey Motor Traction Co Ltd — the first of Hare's overseas ventures, which at one stage included three steamships operating between Millbay, Plymouth

and the Channel Islands. John Hibbs (1968) credits him with latterly having some 250 vehicles under his control.

An agreement with the GWR Road Motor Department in 1925 —by which time DMT had acquired a handful of smaller businesses — had ensured a competition-free environment in the operational areas of both. When the purchase by National was finalised a separate NO&T subsidiary, DMT (1928) Ltd, was set up, and Cdr Hare joined the National board — the vehicles continuing to run in their noticeably different apple-green-and-cream livery — until he decided that life overseas would prove more attractive, whereupon he set up bus services successively in Malta, Egypt and Africa.

*Above:* Valued customers were frequently pursued by manufacturers offering a new model. In 1926 Basingstoke-based John I. Thornycroft Ltd had this new LB model bodied as a 26-seater by preferred coachbuilder Vickers. Painted in DMT green and cream, with larger-than-normal lettering, it went on trial with its intended purchaser but was sold the following year to Venture Ltd, of Basingstoke, thereby avoiding National ownership. *Colin Morris collection*

*Above:* Among the 51 Thornycroft single-deckers included in the sale in 1928 of DMT to the National Omnibus & Transport Co were five 22-seater charabancs, all bodied by Hall Lewis, representing a small but welcome addition to National's West Country touring fleet. What had been DMT No 97 (CO 9457) became NO&T No 2722. *Colin Morris collection*

*Above:* This example of the Bristol 4-ton model, one of 35 similar saloons that passed in 1928 from DMT to National, became the latter's No 2638. CO 7000 and its fellows were fitted with Bristol's own bodywork, representing a combination of chassis and coach bodywork that was to become commonplace in the NO&T fleet and, subsequently, those of Southern and Western National. *Bristol Vintage Bus Group*

*Above:* This Devon Motor Transport Karrier double-decker, CO 2295, pictured on service between Plymouth and Yelverton, would be one of just two buses of that configuration (the other being a Leyland) taken over from DMT by the National Omnibus & Transport Co. Elderly but still robust, what became No 2741 in the National fleet was soon thereafter retired from passenger-carrying duties to become a company lorry. *Alan B. Cross / Noel Jackson collection*

*Above:* Photographed working a Plymouth local service early in Western National days is No 2636 (TA 5610), an ex-Devon Motor Transport Bristol 4-ton model with 30-seat Bristol bodywork. The three WNOC crew members in summer rig look smart enough to have been inspired by the naval tradition of the West Country's most famous port. *Calton Phoenix*

Believed to be No 2534 (DF 4744), initially based at Stroud, Gloucestershire, this Leyland Lion PLSC1 was fitted with 28-seat bodywork by Strachans and delivered to NO&T in 1928. It was later allocated to Falmouth and passed into the Western National fleet. The 'National' fleetname has been applied in the cursive script usually reserved for charabancs. *Southdown Enthusiasts' Club*

National thus found itself operating buses cheek-by-jowl with those of the GWR at a new location — and a large one at that — in addition to similar contact at Bridgwater, Stroud and Weymouth. Discussions between the two operators took place in 1928, and the future area for the forthcoming Western National was set out on paper. Whereas the Southern Railway would simply require that a drawing of one of its railway stations appear on the cover of the Southern National timetable booklets, the Great Western Railway directors asked for something a little more expensive — that all new vehicles for Western National be painted in railway-style chocolate and cream — and for a while got its way. At least the title 'Great Western National' was not discussed — well, not as far as the minutes show!

The Western National Omnibus Co Ltd was registered (as Company No 236066) on 1 January 1929. The share capital at the outset was £1 million, divided into 600,000 6% cumulative preference shares of £1 each and 400,000 ordinary shares at the same amount. The names of the subscribers to the company and holding the nominal one ordinary share each were: F. R. E. Davis, Secretary to the GWR, Bert Smith, General Manager of the NO&T Co Ltd, and the following solicitors' clerks: A. E. Patterson, George Conrad, Arthur D. Gardner, George T. Franks and Charles C. Rose.

According to the Memorandum and Articles of Association, dated 27 December 1928, the objects for which the company was established were primarily (a) 'to acquire and take over as a going concern the businesses of omnibus proprietors

Pictured in its later Western National days (1934) at St Mawes, Cornwall, is No 2864 (DR 5255), a Leyland Tiger TS2 delivered to NO&T in 1928. The dual-door 26-seat 'all-weather' bodywork was built by J. C. Beadle & Co, of Dartford, Kent, which firm was later to undertake a considerable quantity of work for both Southern and Western National. *Alan Lambert collection*

now carried on by the Great Western Railway company and the National Omnibus & Transport Co Ltd, respectively in the counties of Devon and Cornwall and elsewhere', and, in keeping with the military origins of its fleetname, (h) 'to organise and employ any employees of the company and the motor vehicles or other property of the company, into a transport force or forces for military or other purposes'. (Whether the latter was added to the more usual 'objects' because of the General Strike of two years earlier or a dark mistrust of a certain Continental country's intentions is not stated.) Also destined to be of considerable importance later (see Chapter 3) were (b) 'the business

of transport by road in all its branches' and (q) 'to work tramways'.

The number of passenger-service vehicles set to be taken over from NO&T was 225, and from the GWR 115, providing an initial Western National fleet of 340. The new company's operating area was to be initially south and west of Exeter in Devon and in Cornwall south of a line drawn between Okehampton and Newquay which excluded those parts of the west of England served by the Southern Railway company. In the first instance, the allotted territory did not include the road passenger services operated by the two participant founder companies in Gloucestershire, Wiltshire and north Somerset.

# CHAPTER THREE

# GWR and Tilling's Western National

THAT first board meeting of the Western National Omnibus Co Ltd was held at National's headquarters — 206 Brompton Road, London SW3 — on Thursday 21 February 1929. In addition to the Great Western Railway's Superintendent of the Line, R. H. Nicholls, who was indisposed, the following were elected to the WNOC board:

| | |
|---|---|
| Sir John Jarvis Bt | Chairman, National |
| Lord Mildmay of Flete | Director, GWR |
| Henry C. Merrett | Chief Accountant, National |
| James Milne | Chief Accountant, GWR |
| Walter James Iden | Managing Director, National |
| Bert Smith | General Manager, National |

*Below:* No 2916 (DR 5514), one of seven 51-seat open-staircase all-Leyland Titan TD1 models delivered to the National Omnibus & Transport Co in 1929 — which means that these and eight otherwise similar 48-seaters delivered that year remained in two-tone green and cream, even if allotted to Western National upon the division of NO&T's fleet.
*Southdown Enthusiasts' Club*

Messrs Iden, Smith, Cope and F. C. A. Coventry, the GWR's Superintendent of Road Transport (who was invited thereafter to attend the company's board meetings) were appointed as a Committee of Management. The powers of that committee were identical to those set out in respect of the Southern National Omnibus Co, described in the earlier volume on that company (2007). It was decided that, for the time being, the registered office of the new company should remain at National's headquarters in London.

The concerns of that first meeting included the ordering of new vehicles for National (in the interim the operating holding company) — three

Leyland Titans for £5,118, five Leyland Tigers for £7,760 (later amended to two, plus three Titans for £1,700 each) and four AEC Regal saloons for £5,049 — and the transfer to the Western area of six 26-seat Leyland Lioness coaches, at a cost to the National company of £24,163. In the interim the GWR's requirement for 15 Maudslay 32-seat coaches was approved at £17,415.

Also confirmed was the purchase — on behalf of the GWR — of Ashcroft Motors Ltd of Paignton, for £11,000 (although its Torquay–Paignton service was to be worked by Devon General), together with the assets of the West Penwith Omnibus Co Ltd of St Just, also acquired jointly with the GWR, for £4,000. At the same time adjustments were made to ensure that the issue of ordinary £1 shares was equalised between the GWR and NO&T holdings in the new Western National company. The latter's appointed accountants were Messrs Deloitte, Pelender, Griffiths & Co of London.

The need to ensure that those customers booked upon the company's touring and excursion coaches would be given the best possible information about

As the 1930s commenced Leyland's new vehicles displayed an attractive enamelled badge atop the radiator. Leyland Tiger TS2 No 2943 (GF 7291) was fitted with a rakish 26-seat 'sun saloon' body by Hoyal; other Tigers were bodied to the same style by Duple or Strachans. All were memorable for the delightful and homely 'hiss' emitted by their 'wetted gauze' carburettors.
*Andrew Waller collection*

each local feature which rolled one-after-the-other into view was given early consideration. The Managing Committee asked the board (25 March 1929) to approve the purchase of 43 sets of 'Silent Guides' (see illustrations) for fitting to such vehicles in time for the 1929 season, at a cost of £6 10s 0d each. This it duly did, and the system was introduced and used successfully for several years thereafter.

At the same time much thought was given to the way in which stage-carriage competition should be dealt with. It was decided to add to the company's services to make opposition impossible. The GWR was already in a position to exercise considerable influence with certain councils, and the railway company was asked how this influence might best be applied. In one respect particularly the Western National company was in better shape than its Southern counterpart: whereas much time and effort, in the case of the latter, needed to be devoted to the planning and implementation of a whole raft of road/rail interchange connections (the Southern Railway at the time having but one bus, and that inherited from the LSWR), the GWR possessed a very large fleet — and much experience of in-house road/rail connection, which was now placed at the disposal of Western National. However, WNOC made it clear that, where such connecting services were provided at a loss, the GWR would, in principle, be expected to pay half of the deficit.

After a strategic purchase of G. J. Pullen's 'Palace Saloons' of Plymouth — for £7,250 — Western National came to an agreement with HB Buses Ltd and its subsidiary, Cornish Buses Ltd of Truro, which had threatened several WNOC services, a situation compounded when HB (Hopper & Berryman) acquired another route between Plymouth and Totnes. The truce, which at first limited the activities of the opposition and then led to joint running, was reached in July 1929.

In that first year WNOC moved quickly into the property market, purchasing additional land at Camborne for some £6,000 and a garage at Chagford for £700, while the GWR's F. C. A. Coventry engineered a 99-year lease, at a rental of £150 per annum, of the old tin-smelting works in Penzance, together with plans for the erection upon the site of a new garage.

On 7 August 1929 WNOC expanded its area considerably. It purchased from the NO&T Co Ltd the undertaking and assets of its holding company in the Taunton, Trowbridge, Minehead and Stroud areas, for the sum of £140,000, payable in cash on 13 August 1929, the date when completion took place. At the same time WNOC purchased from the GWR its undertaking of the Road Passenger Transport business in the Stroud and Trowbridge areas, for £3,500.

One issue difficult for the National directors to handle was that part of the baggage brought to the table by the GWR — the question of trade-union membership. It was thought desirable to defer recognition of the union for as long as possible but that 'if suitable terms could be arranged with the National Union of Railwaymen [it] should recognise that union in preference to any other. Not until 29 July 1936, however, would an agreement with the NUR finally be signed.

WNOC ended its first year of operations approving the expenditure of £40,000 in 1930 for new rolling stock — and £53,000 on garages and garage extensions. Its profit as at 30 September 1929 had been £28,189.

The 1930 programme contained two items of particular note for those primarily interested in the vehicles used by Western National. In the case of those buses considered no longer suitable for service it was agreed that the GWR should have first refusal of buying them; the fact that four Burford chassis (Nos 808, 857, 870 and 874) were

Strachans' interpretation of the 'in house' body style designed for the Leyland Tigers delivered to Western National in 1930 could be readily identified by the cream relief, which extended to include the window frames (rather than being confined to a simple waistband) and the shallow V-shaped louvres above the opening side windows. Illustrated is one of five (Nos 2947-51) with 26-seat dual-door 'sun saloon' coach bodywork. *Modern Transport*

In 1930, following the purchase by Southern National of two enclosed-staircase 51-seat all-Leyland Titan TD1s, the National companies decided to place the following year's order for bodywork in respect of TD1s with Strachans, two examples of this combination being received by Western National. Oddly the Strachans examples, with just 48 seats apiece, contrived to look larger than the Leyland-bodied version. Trowbridge-based No 3127 (DG 2630) is pictured in World War 2 rig. *The Omnibus Society*

then sold to the railway company at £100 each suggests that they were used thereafter for goods traffic. Secondly, WNOC paid £1,500 for a new and powerful Guy Conquest 26-seat saloon, No 3037 (YD 114), with Hoyal coachwork, for that strenuous Lynton–Minehead route recently acquired from E. E. Porter. The western terminus for this service was actually Lynmouth, passengers being issued with free tickets by WNOC for the journey, up or down, on the Lynton & Lynmouth Cliff Railway — the longest British cliff funicular. And the departed Thomas Clarkson would have been delighted to know that its two cars were propelled solely by the use of water.

An important acquisition finalised in 1931 was that of the Southern General Omnibus Co Ltd and its subsidiary Cornish Buses Ltd, the histories of which have been written in some detail by F. D. Simpson (1980). Southern General had been registered as HB Buses Ltd in March 1929 to take over the business formerly operated as Hopper & Berryman from a garage in St Marybridge Road,

Plymouth. The company was associated with Clarence Mumford, of W. Mumford Ltd — already an important local coachbuilder and, after the dust had settled, destined to produce a considerable quantity of bodywork for both Southern and Western National. In June 1929 HB Buses had bought the business of W. T. Coath & Son's 'Eddystone Motors', of Derry Place, Plymouth, for £2,000 in shares, and in January 1930 acquired bus chassis and bodywork from W. Mumford Ltd for £2,396 in shares and £7,781 in cash and exchange.

After J. H. Watts, of Red & White Services Ltd, had put money into the firm and joined its board of directors, the dovecots at National headquarters had been well and truly fluttered: Red & White had already constrained both National's and Bristol Tramways' efforts to expand in Gloucestershire; had it now plans to do likewise against Western National in Devon? The HB company had become the Southern General Omnibus Co Ltd in February 1930 — much to the chagrin of the London General Omnibus Co Ltd, which protested in vain at the use of its much-prized name (despite the fact that other regional firms had adopted it already). The subsidiary, Cornish Buses, had been registered just three days after HB Buses in 1929, its directors Clarence Mumford and William Simmons-Hodge, who used the 'Cornish' name for the same diplomatic reason as had Devon Motor Transport when it chose to operate west of the River Tamar as 'Cornwall Motor Transport'.

Under the 'Blue Line' fleetname SGOC and Cornish Buses were operating 23 routes at the time of the sale to a relieved Western National — a deal finally completed in August 1931, the total purchase price, at £1 10s 0d (£1.50) per share, being £40,071. In the interim Sir John Jarvis and Messrs Cope, Coventry and Iden had been appointed to the SGOC board, and WNOC had incurred an overdraft in order to finance the purchase. Sixty-three vehicles joined the Western National fleet (Nos 3227-80/6-94), these being of ADC, AEC, Albion, Chevrolet, Ford, Lancia, Morris, Thorny-croft, Vulcan and Willys Overland manufacture — interesting times for the company's fitters.

In 1931 Western National acquired the joint operations (using the 'Blue Line' fleetname) and bus fleet of Southern General and Cornish Buses, in consequence of which an additional 63 vehicles joined the WNOC fleet. One of nine Mumford-bodied AEC Reliances acquired from that source, 32-seat DR 5740 became Western National No 3268. *W.J. Haynes*

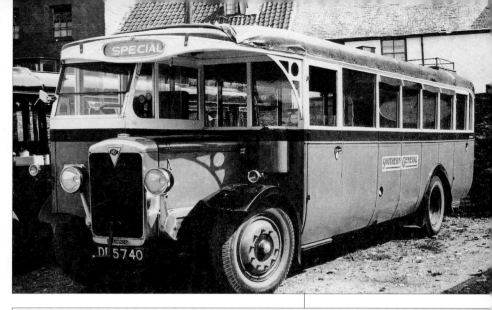

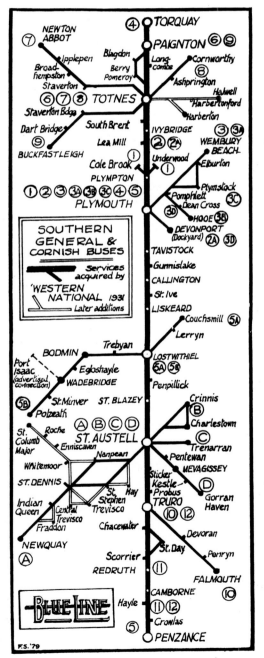

Just four double-deck buses joined the fleet following the acquisition of the 'Blue Line' operation. These were four highbridge Short-bodied AEC Regents. All were re-fitted in 1935 with Gardner six-cylinder oil engines, and No 3272 (DR 6775) was one of three rebodied during World War 2 with 52-seat lowbridge coachwork by Beadle. Postwar it was based at Taunton. *W.J. Haynes*

*Frank Simpson*

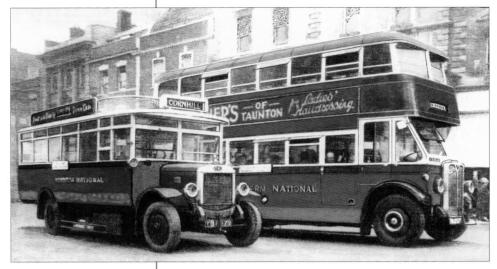

Both local-authority records and directors' minutes reveal that the GWR representatives on WNOC's board preserved chocolate and cream as the fleet livery until late 1931, at least. Thus at Taunton that year ex-NO&T Guy BK/Hickman saloon No 2298 (YB 6479) is pictured alongside new highbridge Short-bodied AEC Regent No 3121 (YD 2527), each in appropriate livery. Artistic licence? Well, just a shade!
*C. Carter / Colin Morris*

During the same period both Southern and Western National companies concerned themselves with the purchase from the parent NO&T of the South Western section of the latter's 'London & Coastal Business', still based at the Shepherd's Bush depot. F. C. A. Coventry of the GWR was nominated WNOC's representative on the proposed Joint Management Committee, the railway company having paid £21,500 as half of the purchase price (this comprising £8,737 for goodwill, £12,444 for rolling stock — 11 coaches — and £319 for a relative proportion of £1 shares in the multi-company London Coastal Coaches Ltd). As a result Western National gained its foothold in express services from London to Devon and Cornwall. Southern National also acquired 11 coaches from the same source, and both companies' South Western express traffic was co-ordinated in order to survive in an area already served by competing firms.

The effects of the Road Traffic Act 1930, whereby Britain was divided into Traffic Areas, are described in the Southern National volume (2007) — as too is in some detail what became the greatest sea-change in the fortunes of the National companies. In

February 1931 Thomas Tilling Ltd purchased a controlling interest in the parent National Omnibus & Transport Co Ltd. As a result the Eastern, Southern and Western National companies were now 50% owned by Tilling.

The change in personnel commenced in April 1932, Henry Merrett and Bert Smith resigning as directors, to be replaced by Tilling's John F. Heaton and George Cardwell. Others would follow in due course. Two further fascinating items occur within the records for that year. Western National came close to purchasing Commander Ryder's Salcombe & Portlemouth Ferry, in order to 'protect the interests of the company', but apparently backed off when it became questionable as to whether WNOC would have gained 'full and proper landing rights'. Secondly, the question of the colours of the company's buses was considered. Any doubt as to whether the first newly ordered Western National buses arrived in GWR chocolate and cream is dispelled by a minute dated 7 August 1931 wherein it is recorded that 'the present chocolate colour had not the wearing properties of the National green. It was desired that estimates in the difference in costs of properly maintaining the vehicles with the present colour and of the National green colour be supplied to members of the board.'

This backs up oft-doubted registration records of some local authorities at the time, which variously describe early WNOC Leylands as being in 'chocolate and cream' or something similar.

In June 1931 WNOC purchased for £3,674 the services and five buses — three REOs, a Dodge and a Gilford (WNOC Nos 3254-8) — of E. E. Piper's 'Red Bus', of Devizes, Wiltshire, thus strengthening a little its presence near its north-eastern boundary. Piper seems to have had a record for popping up in various southern locations, apparently with the

NO&T oversaw the purchase of 12 AEC Regal chassis for Southern/Western National in 1931. WNOC sent one to be bodied by Mumford as a dual-purpose saloon, all the rest being bodied by Beadle as 32-seat coaches. Five of those went to Western National, among them Nos 3113/6 (YD 2301/4), pictured together in as-new condition.
*Andrew Waller collection*

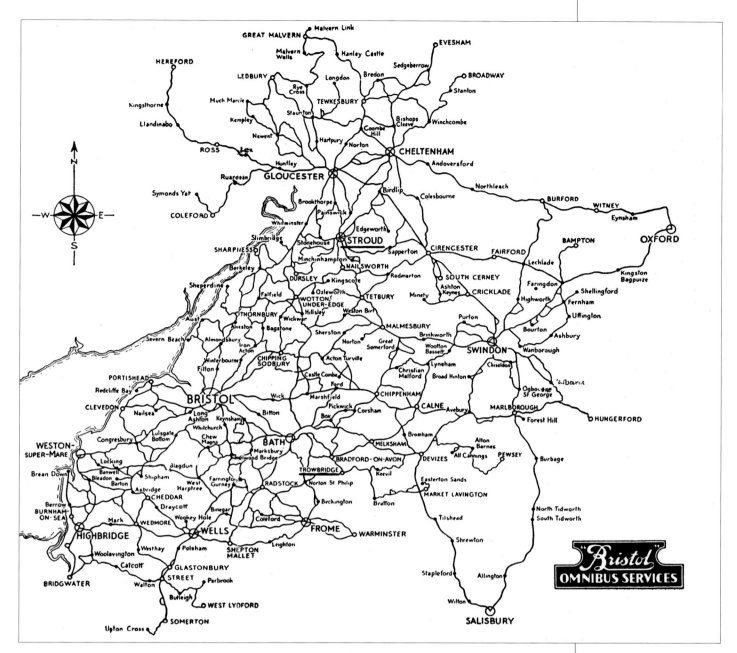

Although depicting the Bristol company's operating area at its post-nationalisation extent and after its change of name (to the Bristol Omnibus Co) this map gives a good idea of the threat held at bay by Western National's two-decade period of control over BTCC affairs. WNOC's Stroud and Trowbridge depots are underlined, to emphasise that threat as finally realised. *Ian Allan Library*

intention of selling up at a profit. Alan Lambert, Chairman of The Omnibus Society's Provincial Historical Research Group, has written a paper about Piper, whom he describes as 'a serial competitor'.

But it was under its new Tilling-influenced management that Western National's most impressive acquisition was to be made. Possibly because the Great Western Railway company realised belatedly that (despite some three years earlier having secured powers to regularise its possession and operation of motor buses) it still did not have powers to involve itself in the running of street tramways, it elected in November 1931 to sell its 50% holding in National's old rival, the Bristol Tramways & Carriage Co Ltd. Both its preference and ordinary shareholdings, each fully paid, were offered to Western National for £1,053,576. Henry Merrett's firm of accountants was instructed to

investigate and report upon the Bristol company's accounts and affairs. Not surprisingly they were found to be in order, and W. J. Iden was authorised to sign an agreement on behalf of Western National. The share capital of the latter was promptly raised from £1 million to £2,083,576 in order to bring about the transaction and leave itself in a position to afford further acquisitions.

The NO&T followed up by first purchasing 3,817 5% shares, 2,440 ordinary shares and 4,906 deferred shares in Bath Electric Tramways Ltd. At the same time the NO&T acquired a mere 320 ordinary shares in Bristol Tramways and presented them free of charge to Western National, thus making it the major shareholder. By this action the Bristol Tramways & Carriage Co Ltd became a subsidiary of the Western National Omnibus Co Ltd.

From April 1932 Walter James Iden and John F. Heaton (an uneasy pairing) joined the board of Bristol Tramways, and from that date WNOC was empowered, if and when requested by the GWR, to nominate other representatives to serve upon the Bristol company's board. Further investments reinforced that position, and the reports, accounts and other matters relating to the Bristol company — and its subsidiaries, the Bath Electric Tramways Ltd and Bath Tramways Motor Co Ltd (the latter owned equally by BT&CC and BET) — became regular items for discussion at the meetings of the Western National board. It was an arrangement destined to survive until 1949. At the outset WNOC authorised a proxy in favour of William G. Verdon Smith and Sir George S. White alternatively for use at the annual general meetings of BT&CC. (An outline of the relationship between

*Above:* The first of four pictures illustrating vehicles operated by WNOC's Bristol Tramways & Carriage Co subsidiary. Pausing in Ledbury, Herefordshire, prior to returning to Gloucester on 7 September 1940 is Bristol B-type No B872 (AHU 958), a 30-seat dual-door saloon built in 1934. As was frequently the case during the early stages of World War 2, only the nearside headlamp has been masked, the bulb on the offside having been removed. *The Omnibus Society*

*Above:* Clutched to BTCC's own bosom, having been put to work by its sister company, the Bristol Aeroplane Co Ltd, was 1934 Bristol-bodied Bristol J-type coach No J130 (AHW 534). This 26-seater, still in blue but with its ivory relief overpainted grey, has both headlamps masked and plenty of white paint at the front to make it visible at ground level in the WW2 blackout. It was used to transport BAC workers to that company's underground factory at Corsham, Wiltshire. *S. L. Poole / London Bus Preservation Group*

*Left:* Delivered at the height of World War 2, in 1942, Bristol K5G No 3626 (HHT 147) was one of eight highbridge 56-seat double-deckers bodied by Bristol itself. Only one delivered separately (with 58 seats) was camouflaged; the others were painted in Bristol Tramways' traditional livery of blue and ivory, as worn by the city's elderly open-top tramcars, until the latter's activities were stopped in their tracks — permanently, as it turned out — by the Luftwaffe. *The Omnibus Society*

members of the White family, Bristol Tramways and the Imperial Tramways group is to be found in *Glory Days: Reading Transport*, published in 2006).

Invited to introduce a reorganisation scheme for both Southern and Western National, in that same month of April 1932 W. J. Iden announced that the registered office of both would be transferred to Exeter and located at 48-50 Queen Street. Four years later the Southern Railway opened negotiations with National for the sale to the latter of 54-58, on the opposite side of the street, and in due course this site came to be well known as National House, Exeter.

Despite the move to Exeter the board meetings, during this period at least, continued to be held in London. The 16th meeting of the company was the first to gather under the Tilling roof at 20 Victoria Street, SW1. It was also the first meeting attended by Percival Stone Clark, Tilling appointee to the post of General Manager of WNOC and, of course, Southern National. He was made responsible for the purchase of materials and for work which, in his opinion, would prove necessary for the proper maintenance of the companies' vehicles, buildings, plant, tools and equipment. He was also to purchase vehicles of any kind, as well as petrol, oil and tyres, and to assume responsibility for vehicle servicing. In addition he was appointed to the renamed Management Committee, in the place of the departed Bert Smith. To help him in matters mechanical David Tuff was appointed as his 'engineering assistant' together with the necessary local staff, William J. Morison remaining Chief Engineer for all three National subsidiaries.

The third local Tilling appointment was of Eric F. Horobin as Traffic Manager. All three were remunerated by the now Tilling-controlled National holding company.

At this point it becomes necessary to explain that Thomas Tilling's interest in the chassis-manufacturing side of the industry began when (as described in Chapter 2) Percy Frost Smith became Manager of its fledgling 'Motor Department', which led to the setting-up of Tilling-Stevens Motors Ltd. This firm had been re-styled 'TS Motors Ltd' in August 1930 as part of a remedial effort to revitalise its fortunes. This version of the firm's title was set to remain in being until 1937, when the company was again renamed, this time as Tilling-Stevens Ltd. In the interests of chronological accuracy, therefore, the following incident in the WNOC story refers to TS Motors Ltd, although readers should be aware that in the 1930s this was a formal shorthand for 'Tilling-Stevens'.

In the summer of 1932 the WNOC board spent a considerable time dealing with developments in relation to its new Bristol subsidiary. In particular, the chassis-manufacturing side of that firm's operations came under close scrutiny from a sub-committee consisting of Iden, Cardwell and Verdon Smith: should the Bristol works be (i) closed down, (ii) developed by the adoption of Bristol vehicles for WNOC and associated companies or (iii) sold to some other manufacturing company?

This hot potato was very much an attempt by J. F. Heaton to rescue the then faltering TS Motors Ltd. His solution was to attempt to form a new company to take over the manufacturing section of the BT&C Co Ltd and amalgamate that with TS Motors Ltd. The terms suggested for taking over the chassis-manufacturing activities of both firms were minuted as follows, being reproduced here exactly; make of them what you will!

*Bristol manufacturing works and plant:*
(a) Lease for a term of years at a rental of, say, £500 per annum
(b) One half of profits after provision for certain dividends
(c) supply of vehicles and spare parts to the Bristol company and the Western National company at cost plus 10%, any maintenance work done on behalf of the Bristol company being on similar terms

*TS Motors Ltd goodwill, machinery, plant and certain other assets:*
(d) 100,000 5% preference shares of £1 each, without voting rights, guaranteed up to a period of five years by the National company
(e) a cash payment of £20,000-£50,000. The new company, at the outset, would issue:—
(f) the 100,000 preference shares above mentioned [and] 50,000 ordinary shares of £1 each for cash at par to the National company or its nominees

[The above accurate record was duly signed as such by Heaton at the next WNOC board meeting. The 'National company' in this instance refers to the holding company, the National Omnibus & Transport Co Ltd.]

Pictured postwar in Tilling-inspired green and cream are two contrasting vehicles, both, however, looking distinctly 'Bristol fashion'. A 1941 Bristol K5G/ECW highbridge double-decker, No C3316 (GHT 128), of Bristol Joint Services — managed jointly by BTCC and the Corporation — stands beside a rare 1937 Dennis Mace/Duple dual-purpose saloon (one of only six), No 654 (DHY 650), of Bristol Country Services. *The Omnibus Society*

An unusual purchase in 1932 was of five Dennis Lancets with 32-seat bus bodywork by Beadle. No 3373 (JY 90) was the first; originally petrol-engined, it was fitted four years later with a four-cylinder Gardner unit. It spent most of its career based at Taunton, Somerset, where its 'intermediate size' seating capacity proved very useful. *W. J. Haynes*

A warning shot was then fired across the bows of this raft of ideas by the GWR's Sir James Milne, who reminded the WNOC board that 'the railway company would have to consider the effect of the provision restrictive of interest in the manufacture of chassis in the Great Western Railway Act of 1928'. By this interjection Sir James may well be said to have ensured the future production of all those thoroughbred Bristol vehicles which thereafter graced the roads of Britain and elsewhere.

Mindful of just how it had acquired its majority shareholding in the Bristol company in the first place, the board of Western National sat on the fence: '… if the board of the Bristol Tramways company consider it desirable to acquire the assets of TS Motors Ltd … no objection should be raised by this company'. Whether· it would have dared to do that to the formidable J. F. Heaton just a few

years hence is rather questionable. The board of the BT&CC did not so decide. In the event, the products of TSM were simply seen off by the excellence of the Bristol vehicles. Thomas Tilling Ltd instead threw its weight behind the production of Bristol-built chassis — and disposed of its shareholding in Tilling-Stevens. The latter staggered on in decline until 1953, when vehicle production finally ceased. Not for the last time, Heaton had demonstrated that he was primarily a businessman rather than an engineer.

At a time when WNOC had not yet gained control of the whole of the GWR's Road Motor interests, the decision *vis à vis* the latter's buildings was that it would be in the company's best interest to close down the railway's smaller sheds, repair work being instead concentrated in certain main depots. Although considerable economies would result thereby, 'certain employees would become redundant'. Whether the recording of such a concern represented philanthropic anxiety or plain matters of fact is unclear.

After Southern National had negotiated the purchase of Chaplin & Rogers' Chard Motors in 1932, an arrangement was made for Western National to contribute £1,979, representing its interest in the road thence to Taunton. It was apportioned as follows: two public-service vehicles (Star Flyer YC 6503 and Chevrolet LO YC 7637) £435; goodwill £1,544.

In November 1932 J. F. Heaton took the chair for the first time — as a holding measure only — whilst as part of an in-house GWR arrangement F. C. A. Coventry was at last given a seat proper upon the board, in place of Lord Mildmay of Flete. Sir John Jarvis and Walter J. Iden resigned and were replaced respectively by Tilling's Stanley Kennedy and Percy Stone Clark. George Cardwell replaced Iden upon the Management Committee. In a diplomatic move, the latter's place on the board of BT&CC was allotted to F. C. A. Coventry. Crawley and Simpson (1990) relate how Iden, who had done so much to fashion the structure and ethos of NO&T and its operating subsidiaries, was allotted an office at Tilling's London headquarters — and given next to nothing to do. Such disrespect was not what he deserved.

On the vehicle side, elderly, high-framed chassis were now due for disposal. No-one in the bus industry wanted them. Indeed, the demand for such chassis was so low that, instead of receiving reports of the sum they had realised upon sale, the board was presented with the cost of scrapping them.

Of the 17 vehicles from Eli Dunn's Taunton-based fleet that joined Western National in 1933 just two were double-deckers. Both were Dennis Lance models seating 52 passengers; whilst one had open-staircase bodywork by Strachans, the other — WNOC 3440 (YD 3862) — had a more modern fully enclosed structure by Duple. *Alan Lambert collection*

Dunn's fleet was extremely varied — and correspondingly difficult to maintain. Represented therein were 11 chassis-type variations and nine different makes of bodywork. Besides the two double-deckers was this unique Morris Commercial Dictator — YD 4649 — with Midland Counties 35-seat dual-purpose bodywork, which became Western National No 3442.
*The Omnibus Society*

Despite results generally for the financial year ending 30 September 1932 having proven so poor that they were withheld from general publication (proof indeed that there were no shareholders other than Tilling-owned NO&T and the GWR), the coming financial year saw WNOC find sufficient funds to resume the process of expansion by acquisition. This way forward, which gained momentum as the year progressed, began with a purchase in Taunton, where the company bought Thomas Motors Ltd, bringing seven vehicles (two Albions, two Lancias, two Leylands and a Morris Dictator), for £12,000. The price also included a taxi business, which was quickly sold on (for £412). Destined to take somewhat longer was the reeling-in of an even bigger fish based in the county town of Somerset — the services and vehicles (nine Leyland single-deckers, two Lancia, two Maudslay and two Morris single-deckers and two Dennis Lance double-deckers) of Eli Dunn's bus business. This was to lead to Dunn's briefly holding the position of WNOC's Area Traffic Superintendent, based at what had been his own premises in Taunton. Before those premises, in what WNOC continued to call Bridgwater Road (although its name had changed just previously), had been actually conveyed to the company, plans were afoot to extend them and incorporate Dunn's eight services into the existing series.

The 20th meeting of the WNOC board, on December 1932, brought about a unique situation whereby membership of the Southern National and Western National boards of directors was not exactly the same. Tilling's J. F. Heaton had become Chairman of Southern National, but a memorandum under seal by the Great Western Railway was presented which nominated to the WNOC board Bristol's William G. Verdon Smith, to take the place of GWR's R. H. Nicholls. Verdon Smith was duly appointed a director — and immediately elected to the role of Chairman of the Western National Omnibus Co Ltd, whilst still retaining his role within its BT&CC subsidiary.

The GWR's Chief Accountant (and WNOC director) Ralph Cope had by this time been in preliminary touch with the Elliott brothers of Bournemouth, proprietors of Royal Blue Automobile Services. Cope reported that the Elliotts 'desired to see Mr Heaton' on the matter of a possible purchase of their business. Heaton promptly warmed to their bravery by announcing a tad loftily that he 'would be prepared to meet them'. What followed over the next two years led of course to Southern/Western National's (and Hants & Dorset's) acquisition and adoption of the classic and stylish 'Royal Blue' brand. Those events are described in some detail in *Glory Days: Royal Blue* (2000) and in Chapter 5 of *Southern National Omnibus Company* (2007).

A fascinating minute of the same period notes that F. C. A. Coventry had been to see John Watts (or Secretary Guy Bown) of Red & White Services Ltd 'to ascertain how far Mr Cownie's conversations had proceeded'. William Cownie, Managing Director of the National Electric Construction Co Ltd, had died earlier in December 1932, but it would seem that NECC, parent company of, among others, the Devon General Omnibus & Touring Co Ltd, had made tentative enquiries about a possible purchase of all or part of Red & White. So too had Western National, for the following July it negotiated (unsuccessfully) for a takeover of its operations in the Stroud area. At length, in November 1933, WNOC and Red & White entered into a working and pooling agreement for the Stroud district, in which they had previously competed.

In 1933 Western National 'thought about' acquiring the shares and assets of Bath Electric Tramways Ltd and its subsidiary, the Bath Tramways Motor Co. In the main it was left to the Bristol Tramways company to do so. This was also a period when those independents who had survived the initial impact of the Road Traffic Act 1930 began to sell part or all of their road-transport businesses. In short order, purchases for the following were confirmed: Broming, Totnes (£725), Chalk, Torpoint (£30), Mrs M. M. Williams' Embankment Motor

In the aftermath of Heaton's last-ditch defence of TSM — and the resultant triumph of the Bristol chassis — all new examples of the former which went west were delivered to Southern National; as appropriate to its BTCC connection, Western National received its first new Bristol chassis. The first nine of that 1933 intake of 32-seat saloons were bodied by Bristol, the remainder by Brush. No 135 (FJ 8965) was one of 30 Brush-bodied Bristol H types. *Colin Morris collection*

Services, Plymouth (stage only, £7,500), Ford, of Alcombe, Minehead (£1,750), Hanks, Bishops Lydeard (£2,300), Marazion Services, Marazion (£5,000), Oxenham, Lynmouth (£125), Williams, Watchet (£3,000), and Zenith Motor Services, Plymouth (£6,890). The most important acquisition at this time, however, was of the aforementioned Dunn's Services, Taunton, for £31,000. Gaining this wide range of services led to an example of how the Southern and Western National companies' interests differed to the point of outright disagreement. One of the newly acquired routes ran from Taunton to Seaton. 'South of Honiton — that's our territory,' said Southern National; 'the service should be run jointly!' Bearing in mind that the two National directors were the same for both companies, one must presume that the GWR representatives rather enjoyed this step across the Southern Railway's spinal line to the West Country. It was not until April 1934 that WNOC agreed to let Southern

*Upper left:* In 1934 Western National discovered that there was available on the market an extraordinarily agile new bus, with sprightly performance and a 40ft turning-circle. The latter had been achieved by placing the front axle behind the engine, the visual effect leading to the type's nickname of 'flying pig'. It was known more properly as the Dennis Ace, No 700 (OD 7789) being the first. *Colin Morris collection*

*Lower left:* The 20-seat bodywork on No 700 and its 34 companions in the 1934 batch — all of which went to Western National — was by Eastern Counties, of Lowestoft. A luggage rack and outstanding forward visibility are notable features of this interior view. *Colin Morris collection*

National participate — on payment of £250. The latter retaliated by charging WNOC 2s 6d (12½p) per vehicle for storage at Okehampton. Elsewhere in 1933 WNOC took over the Burnham-on-Sea section of the business run by Burnell, of Weston-super-Mare, now acquired by the Bristol subsidiary.

Another area of discord between SNOC and WNOC surfaced that year when a previously agreed pooling arrangement between the two for services from London to the West Country was scuppered by the latter. Fortunately it was replaced by a larger pooling agreement involving Elliott Bros (Bournemouth) Ltd, which included the latter's London–Bournemouth and London–Plymouth routes — 'operated by this company and Elliott Bros', according to the WNOC board minute, which includes the fascinating pencilled insertion 'and by the Southern National company'.

The effective demotion (one way or the other) of the original NO&TC personnel by Tilling saw H. G. R. Lambert and Roland Buszard lose their (now discontinued) offices as district managers, to be transferred to Exeter HQ, the former as Operating Manager, at a reduced salary; the same applied to the latter when he became Assistant Traffic Manager. In this instance, however, both survived with the company, Buszard being appointed Traffic Manager (Operating) in 1944 and serving thus until 1952.

The year 1933 closed with further operational purchases. These included Metford Day, Nether Stowey (£2,000), the Uley–Dursley service (ex Scadding) from BT&CC (£450), part of the business ex Thorpe, Stroud, from Red & White Services (£202), Dartmouth & District Bus Co (£850), C. T. Ridgmont, Westonzoyland (vehicle only, £75), and a most significant purchase in terms of future express services — the acquisition from the receiver of Highways (Bournemouth) Ltd, for £7,742. The latter led to closing negotiations for the purchase of both Elliott Bros (Bournemouth) Ltd's Royal Blue and Tourist Motor Coaches (Southampton) Ltd — for which see *Glory Days: Royal Blue* (2000), *Southern National Omnibus Co* (2007) and a forthcoming volume, *Royal Blue Days*.

A further clutch of acquisitions were made in 1935: Glanville, Taunton (£1,350), an Excursions & Tours licence from Trembath, Kingsbridge (£25), Red Car Motor Co, Stithians (£3,000), and a half-share in the express services of A. E. Good, Seaton, whose firm had recently been purchased by SNOC for £7,500. At the end of the year Percy Stone Clark, the General Manager, was 'posted' by Tilling from Exeter to London. The position was awarded to Bernard Venn Smith, Claude H. J. Pickett becoming Secretary and Assistant General Manager. One of the benefits of WNOC's Bristol connection was a bonus of £260,000 received during the 1936/7 financial year from BT&CC and placed in the WNOC general fund. The company continued to purchase Bristol shares, gaining a further 14,000 that year.

Acquisitions in 1938 included those from: Truscott Bros, of Rilla Mill, Callington (£6,375) Heard & Son,

Timberscombe (£3,610), Richards, of Kenwyn, Truro (£3,400), Truscott, Liskeard (£300) and the sales business and beach service of Riders Garage, Falmouth (£15,450). The year closed with Claude Pickett being replaced as Secretary by Henry J. Downs.

In the final months before the outbreak in September 1939 of World War 2 WNOC looked upon the bright side: the capital of the company was raised from £2,183,576 to £2,400,000, a proposed new bus station for Bridgwater was discussed, and a site at Lemon Quay, Truro, was acquired, for £5,000; the purchase from the Southern Railway of Nos 54-58 Queen Street, Exeter was finally confirmed, and a rolling-stock programme for 1940 was announced. This called for seven Bristol K5G/ECW 56-seat double-deckers (all delivered that next year), 13 Bristol L5G/BBW 31-seat saloons (12 delivered) and 13 Bedford OB/Duple 26-seat luxury coaches (only eight, not surprisingly) — altogether not too bad, compared with the lot of operators elsewhere. The last prewar acquisitions involved the licences for four stage-carriage services run by Herbert and Paul Rosewarne, of Porthleven (£2,900) and T. W. Billington's two saloon buses (£950), the rent of his garage at Saltash and his employment by WNOC — an arrangement brought to a dramatic halt by some erratic bombing by the Luftwaffe in 1941.

*Top and above:*
Also entering service with Western National in 1934 and bodied by Eastern Counties were the first examples of the forward-control version of the Ace — the Dennis Mace. In 1936 they were followed by seven bodied by Brush, one of these being 622 (BUO 795).
The advantage of siting the driver in isolation beside the engine lay in the fact that six extra seats could be provided. Two of the Mace's six extra seats replaced the Ace's luggage rack, these and a further four facing rearwards against the front bulkhead rendering the Mace a 26-seater. But where was the conductor supposed to stand? *Colin Morris collection (both)*

*Above:* A photograph symbolising the disagreements that surfaced between Southern and Western National. In 1936 the former bought Sully's Service, of Chard, Somerset, along with five services and 11 vehicles. Western National complained, insisting upon joint working on three services, and 'bagged' three 32-seat Dennis Lancets. Beadle-bodied No 3643 (YD 6986), here parked at Taunton, was one of them. *The Omnibus Society*

*Above:* As earlier Western National vehicles were found to be still in good shape mechanically in the late 1930s a considerable number had their chassis sent for rebodying. It says much for the products of Leyland Motors that its 'long' Lion PLSC3 was considered a strong candidate for such treatment. Bodied originally by Beadle, No 2602 (VW 4710) received this 32-seat Mumford replacement in May 1936. It is pictured *en route* for Helston. *D. C. Fisk / Alan B. Cross collection*

*Above:* Delivered new to the National Omnibus & Transport Co in 1927 with 26-seat bodywork by Strachan & Brown, this Leyland Lioness PLC1 joined the Western National fleet in 1929 as a service bus. In July 1936, however, No 2341 (VW 194) became the last of its batch to be rebuilt by W. Mumford as an 'all weather' coach, sporting a cream livery with green waistband and 'winged wheel' motifs. *The Omnibus Society*

*Right:* Perhaps inspired by Hants & Dorset's newly repainted green-and-cream coaches of the same year, in 1937 Southern and Western National adopted this 'reverse image' of the H&D scheme. New in 1929 with Strachans bodywork and based originally at Trowbridge, Wiltshire, Leyland Lion PLSC No 2843 (MW 4154) received this Mumford body in February 1937 and was sent to Truro, Cornwall, its 'button nose' radiator by now looking somewhat dated. *The Omnibus Society*

*Left:* 'When I was going to St Ives …' AEC Regal No 2962 (YC 9724) was one of four Strachans-bodied saloon buses delivered to Western National in 1930 for use at Taunton. Having been fitted in December 1937 with this attractive 32-seat dual-purpose body by Beadle, it was sent to Cornwall, an area better suited to this more versatile configuration. *Andrew Waller collection*

*Right:* Delivered just before the outbreak of World War 2 was this Bedford WTB with 25-seat Duple coachwork, No 426 (DDV 26), the 4xx number series having been allotted to this type in 1937.
In common with the rest of the 1939 batch of WTBs it was fitted with the style of radiator that would later be adopted for the OB, distinguishable by the high mounting of the headlamps — although this set looks particularly high. Pictured in its latter days, No 426 was working postwar on the shuttle service between Penzance railway station and the heliport. *Peter Yeomans*

Among the vehicles loaned to Western National for much of World War 2 by the Brighton, Hove & District Omnibus Co were three AEC Regents with BH&D's own open-top bodywork. In 1942 they were sent to ECW to be fitted with removable roofs. Parked beside WNOC's Taunton office in 1943 is BH&D No 6004 (GJ 2004), with paper sticker indicating its destination of Wellington. *The Omnibus Society*

Following the declaration of war, on 3 September 1939, all building projects were set aside. Fearing immediate air attacks upon London, senior Tilling officers vacated Crewe House, their HQ in Curzon Street, and took up residence at Bovington Grange, Hertfordshire, where WNOC's 54th board meeting was held on 17 November. By February 1940, there having been no immediate air raids, they returned to Crewe House, and future board meetings were held both there and at 104 Park Street, London W1.

Western National's war began in earnest in October 1940, when two of its single-deck vehicles were destroyed at Houndstone Camp, in Somerset. Far worse was to come: just as the Luftwaffe had attacked the docks at both Southampton and Portsmouth in careless fashion and done far worse damage to the civil and commercial areas of both cities, so planned attacks upon Devonport Dockyard did far worse destruction in the city of Plymouth itself. As Lord and (to a greater extent, the transatlantic tones of) Lady Astor did their best to raise the spirits of a shaken citizenry came the devastating night attack of 21 March 1941 — just after the King and Queen had paid a morale-boosting visit. Having suffered a largely incendiary attack, the city burned for almost a fortnight. That night 50 WNOC vehicles were either destroyed or put out

of action when a high-explosive bomb scored a direct hit upon the company's garage at Laira Bridge Road. Another attack on 21 April put paid to another seven vehicles at the same location. A large-scale night-time dispersal of buses followed, and the major engineering facility was removed to SNOC's Bideford depot for the rest of the war (see Morris 2007). This troubled period is described in considerable detail by Crawley and Simpson (1990).

The first replacement vehicles brought in (during March) were the BH&D AEC Regents identified in the Introduction to this book. Western National also attempted to fill the gap by hiring vehicles from Plymouth Corporation, but, rather than help provide the necessary transport facilities for local people, the Council elected to play a political card: the city's public purse would not be raided to help a profit-making company. Brighton, Hove & District helped as much as it could by sending a total of 10 AEC Regent double-deckers to augment seven new Bristol K5G/ECW buses delivered that year, and vehicles were transferred from other depots in the West Country — not an easy task, numerous WNOC buses having been requisitioned for use by the military.

Plymouth Corporation now sought to benefit from WNOC's predicament by lodging applications, dated 3 June 1941, with the Regional Transport Commissioner for the South Western Area to provide 10 services from Plymouth to points outside the Corporation boundary. Ten days later the Commissioner refused all 10 applications. Early the following December J. F. Heaton met the Regional Commissioner, Sir Alfred Robinson, together with representatives of Plymouth Corporation — and presented proposals for pooling receipts on certain services of both WNOC and the Corporation operated in the Plymouth area; it would appear that the Commissioner had knocked a few heads together. Thus was born the long-lived 'Plymouth

Joint Services' agreement, eventually covering 100 route variations. Such a notion originally stemmed from a 'tramway protection' scheme, set up in 1932, whereby WNOC had paid the Corporation a percentage of receipts taken within the city. This had been followed in 1936 by a proposal for a merger of the company's and the Corporation's passenger-transport interests within a 15-mile radius of Plymouth. Negotiations failed within months, but it was suggested that they 'might be reopened at a later date'. It had taken some time! The joint committee met for the first time on 7 September 1942 — and joint running commenced 24 days later.

Also in 1942 Heaton (now Sir Frederick) reported that eight producer-gas vehicles were in operation and that 22 more would be 'arriving in the near future'. Such a method of propulsion was imposed upon bus operators nationwide, and Heaton pursued its application with enthusiasm. Inboard varieties having failed, he coaxed National's William Morison into designing an anthracite-burning trailer, to be attached to each selected bus. This Morison did (secretly reckoning that he could have done much better with one powered by steam), and it was produced and marketed as planned by Bristol as the 2T2. The idea was to save petrol for the war effort, but the reality was that, when confronted by the slightest of hills, these vehicles simply held up military convoys assembling during the build-up to D-Day. (For illustrations see *Southern National Omnibus Company*.)

*Above:* Pausing at St Andrew's Cross *en route* from Plymstock to Torpoint Ferry is No 259 (ETT 953), a 1938 Bristol L5G/Mumford 31-seat saloon with seats rearranged in perimeter fashion to accommodate a greater number of standing passengers — a WW2 measure. Two Leyland Titans of Plymouth City Transport represent the municipality's contribution to this 1943 PJS scene. The wreckage between this point and the ruined Charles Church (centre) would become the site of Breton Side bus station, opened in 1958. *Ian Allan Library*

*Above:* Parked beside Laira Bridge garage in March 1943 is Bristol K5G No 249 (ETA 972), on a Plymouth Joint Services working between Saltash Passage and Plymstock. Its original Beadle body, badly damaged in the March 1941 bombing of these premises, appears to have retained its highbridge configuration upon rebuilding by ECW in 1942. The depot's decorative façade would finally succumb to the attentions of the Luftwaffe in April 1944, when three company 'fire watchers' were killed and three injured at the garage entrance. *Ian Allan Library*

*Above:* William J. Morison, pictured in his last decade with the National organisation, had worked with Thomas Clarkson, the National Steam Bus Co, NO&T and its Eastern, Southern and Western National subsidiaries; now, during World War 2, at Heaton's behest, he designed the anthracite-powered T2T gas trailer — built by WNOC's Bristol subsidiary — to be attached to suitably converted buses nationwide. (For an illustration see *Southern National Omnibus Company*, published 2007.) *D. W. Morison / Colin Morris*

As part of a scheme first mooted in 1942, WNOC the following year entered into the Tilefer Contract, whereby knocked-down and imported jeeps for the British, Canadian and US armies were to have been assembled at what remained of the company's Laira

Bridge works. Perhaps, therefore, there was some justification for the second ravaging attack upon the premises on the night of 30 April 1944, just five weeks before the invasion of Normandy was launched. On this occasion three fire-watching employees were killed, and three seriously injured — and 42 company vehicles were damaged or destroyed. Heavy rain thereafter made recovery work extremely difficult. Of the 24 WNOC employees killed in all theatres of WW2, 10 had been based at the company's Plymouth depot.

In September 1944 F. C. A. Coventry, the long-serving GWR director, died. He was replaced upon the board by the railway company's Archibald Dent, and, at the end of the year, George J. Brown became Chief Engineer. By December the Allies were

*Above:* Perhaps surprisingly, given the danger posed by enemy air attacks upon large buildings, a considerable amount of vehicle refurbishment was carried out during World War 2. Having already (in 1937) received a Gardner five-cylinder oil engine, No 156 (OD 7841), a Bristol H new in 1934, had its 32-seat Eastern Counties body attended to by ECW in 1943, although only the side windows would appear to have been updated. *Peter Yeomans*

*Left:* In uncamouflaged World War 2 guise in June 1943, AEC Regent No 3269 (CV 1829) waits to depart Taunton for Burnham-on-Sea. One of four such buses (with highbridge Short Bros bodywork) acquired in 1931 with the Blue Line fleet, it had been fitted in 1935 with a Gardner six-cylinder engine (hence the bulging radiator), gaining this lowbridge Beadle body in April 1943. *S. L. Poole / London Bus Preservation Group*

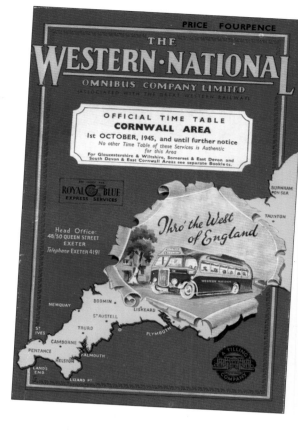

sufficiently confident of victory in Europe to set up a Control Commission for Germany (Transportation Division), and WNOC Traffic Manager Eric Horobin was 'borrowed' to help plan the commission's British contribution. He was paid the honour of being replaced by two officers — Roland Buszard as Traffic Manager (Operating) and Clement Preece as Traffic Manager (Commercial). The GWR's Sir Ralph Cope resigned as a director on 20 December 1945, to be replaced by that company's Cyril R. Dashwood.

To facilitate the return of the WNOC 'central works' from Bideford to Plymouth it was decided in February 1946 to build an extension to the Laira Bridge premises, at a cost of £6,000. More significant in terms of expenditure was the vehicle order for 1947, which called for:

| | | |
|---|---|---|
| 20 | 55-seater Bristol K/ECW double-deckers | £54,000 |
| 13 | 20-seater Bedford luxury coaches | £16,900 |
| 13 | 32-seater Bristol luxury coaches for Royal Blue | £35,000 |
| 24 | 35-seater Bristol omnibus bodies | £26,400 |
| 2 | 32-seater Royal Blue luxury coach bodies | £2,500 |
| 3 | 32-seater service-coach bodies | £53,700 |
| 7 | Gardner engines for oil-engine conversions | £2,100 |

One of the last acts of those WNOC directors representing the Great Western Railway company, prior to its nationalisation, was to participate in a discussion about the pay of the General Manager and Secretary. Whereas previously these gentlemen had been officially employees of the NO&TC, as from 1 May 1947 they were to be transferred to the direct employment of the WNOC and SNOC conjointly. B. V. Smith and H. L. Ellis were thereby added to the monthly salaried staff. There followed information that a separate company, to be called Bristol Commercial Vehicles Ltd, was to be set up — and that, as far as GWR's Sir James Milne and Archibald Dent were concerned, was that!

Delivered for World War 2 service from Trowbridge was Western National's first bus with bodywork built to strictly 'utility' specification and fitted with slatted wooden seats — ideal for drying-out saturated Army greatcoats, as well as reducing manufacturing costs. A Bristol K5G/Duple 55-seater delivered in 1942, No 348 (GTA 392) was one of three gratefully received that year.
*The Omnibus Society*

*Left:* Seven utility-standard Guy Arab 5LW double-deckers with 55-seat Northern Counties bodywork joined the Western National fleet in 1942/3. Of lowbridge configuration, they were less than ideally suited to working in Plymouth, where they were largely employed. No 83 (HTA 886) was photographed (perhaps unkindly, as it needed a wash) postwar working joint route 95A, the demanding cross-city service between Plymstock and Saltash Passage. *S. N. J. White / Andrew Waller collection*

*Right:* In 1942/3 both Southern and Western National took delivery of the wartime Bedford OWB saloon, in a ratio of 10 to 20. All were bodied by Duple and had standard utility features, including 32 wooden-slatted seats. In this summer scene, recorded at Penzance on 1 August 1952, WNOC No 444 (DOD 542), still in original livery, is *en route* for Mousehole ('Mowzle'). Beside it, in typical postwar Tilling green with two cream bands, Bristol KSW6B/ECW No 1815 (LTA 834) prepares to depart for Camborne. *Alan B. Cross*

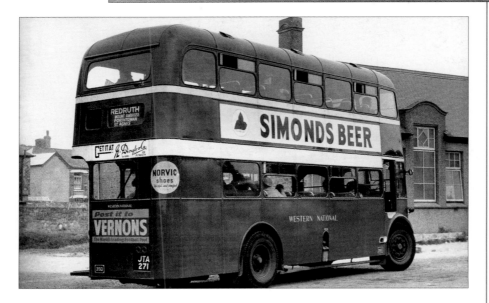

*Left:* Photographed at Perranporth on 20 July 1952, No 350 (JTA 271) had been WNOC's only Bristol delivery of 1943. It was, however, very special in that it bore Eastern Coach Works' prototype highbridge body (perpetuated, in modified form, on postwar deliveries), designed to seat 56 passengers. As depicted here it has retained ECW's early 'hit and miss' sliding-window arrangement but has been repainted in standard postwar Tilling livery. *Peter G. Davey*

# The BTC's and THC's Western National

It took bus builders nation-wide some considerable time to replace their wartime activities with normal peacetime production. In the interim, for bus operators it was a time of make do and mend. Coachbuilders were ready before chassis manufacturers, so rebodying the old went into overdrive. Western National No 3335 (FJ 7835), a Leyland TD1 bought from Exeter Corporation in 1945, was rebodied by Beadle in 1947 and given this Covrad radiator to make it look more modern.
*The Omnibus Society*

A popular Beadle body among numerous Tilling Group subsidiaries was this 1947 style, designed specifically for rebodying elderly chassis. An unusual characteristic was the replication of its large destination display at the rear of the saloon but below cantrail level — a feature copied thereafter by several other coachbuilders. This Leyland Lion LT2, originally fitted with Leyland's own bodywork, was purchased from Eastern Counties in 1945. No 3366 (VE 4805) was rebodied thus two years later. *Alan B. Cross*

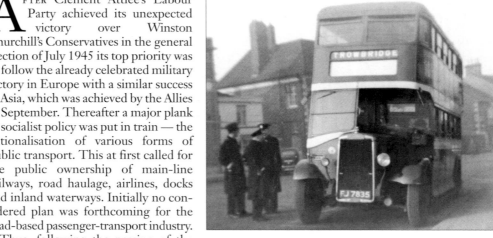

AFTER Clement Attlee's Labour Party achieved its unexpected victory over Winston Churchill's Conservatives in the general election of July 1945 its top priority was to follow the already celebrated military victory in Europe with a similar success in Asia, which was achieved by the Allies in September. Thereafter a major plank of socialist policy was put in train — the nationalisation of various forms of public transport. This at first called for the public ownership of main-line railways, road haulage, airlines, docks and inland waterways. Initially no considered plan was forthcoming for the road-based passenger-transport industry.

Thus, following the passing of the Transport Act 1947, only one third (or, in the case of Eastern, Southern and Western National, one half) of each territorial bus company was earmarked for state ownership — that owned hitherto by one or more of the main-line railway companies. On 1 January 1948 the latter became the concern of the newly constituted British Transport Commission. The Great Western Railway was thereby transformed into British Railways (Western Region) — a situation not too unfamiliar for its management and staff, not least since from the onset of World War 2 and until 1947, all four main-line railway companies had been run as part of the wartime Railway

Executive. From January 1948, therefore, one half of all three National Omnibus & Transport Co's subsidiaries were tucked into the British Transport Commission's portfolio.

On 17 February 1948 it was announced that the GWR's Western National directors, Sir James Milne and A. E. C. Dent, had resigned, to be replaced upon the board by representatives of British Railways (Western Region). At the same time, and as a result of the Government's having called in Thomas Tilling Ltd to organise and run the BTC's Road Transport Executive, George Cardwell temporarily departed from the board of

Western National (and other Tilling-associated companies) to design and lay down the foundation of the RTE. His task largely performed, he was to return the following year as Chairman of both Southern and Western National.

Cardwell had been appointed Chairman to replace the longest-serving officer to hold that position, Sir Frederick Heaton (16 years with Southern National and 13 with Western National). Heaton at the time of his departure had been chairman of 21 Tilling Group bus companies and nine in other fields. Percy Stone Clark and C. R. Dashwood resigned as directors of Western National at the same time.

In June 1949 arrangements were made for Western National's shareholdings in the Bristol Tramways & Carriage Co Ltd to be transferred to what had become Tillings Transport (BTC) Ltd. In exchange £4,879,636 of the BTC's 3% guaranteed stock was earmarked for transfer to Western National and backdated to 1 April 1949. However, from September of that year prior approval had to be sought from the Tilling Executive for certain types of capital expenditure and other commitments.

Following Southern and Western National's choice of Beadle of Dartford for the construction of bodywork for some of their first Royal Blue coaches in 1935, numbers of other coach and saloon bodies postwar and Southern National's prototype Beadle-Leyland saloon (No 2000) of 1946, Major F. J. Chapple and Bernard Venn Smith were asked to look into the matter of the hire and possible purchase of a chassisless Beadle-Sentinel saloon. That vehicle became No 2006 (HOD 57) in the Western National fleet — a one-off which was followed by a dozen Beadle-Bedford chassisless units and two Beadle-Morris examples (plus five Beadle-Bedfords for Southern National), all delivered by the end of 1949.

The process of obtaining reparation for World War 2 losses proved to be a lengthy one. In September 1949 settlement in relation to the severe damage inflicted upon Laira Bridge Road garage, Plymouth, had been reached with the War Damage Commission at £25,479. Two months later, revised plans and modifications including an enlarged office block, altered entrances, a canteen building and increased concrete forecourts came to £28,000 above 'the works claim'. At the same time extensions and improvements were put in train for Falmouth garage and the construction of the bus station and garage at Lemon Quay, Truro, and the bus station at Tower Lane, Taunton. The year ended with Western National purchasing (for £95) that part of the services previously operated by Greenslades Tours Ltd in the agreed territory of WNOC recently acquired, the rest of Greenslades' stage-carriage work passing to the Devon General company.

Postwar, Tilling had planned to provide its subsidiaries with a standard, easily maintained pair of engineer's buses — Bristol's K-type double-decker and L-type saloon, both with 'Series 2' bodywork by Eastern Coach Works — but sheer demand necessitated some diversification. Nevertheless, Western National's first buses to the desired pattern arrived in 1946. No 818 (HTT 989), a K5G, was one of the 1947 batch and became a regular performer on the Trowbridge–Devizes route. *Peter Yeomans*

When orders proved beyond the capacity of Bristol it was Tilling that decided upon the choice of alternative suppliers. Leyland Motors was delighted to fall into this category in 1947, when 12 Titan PD1A chassis were ordered for Western National (along with four for Southern National). Here No 2924 (JUO 951), with 53-seat ECW body, returns to Plymouth from Torquay. *Ian Allan Library*

In 1948 Bristol's output of single-deck chassis was also limited, so 12 AEC Regal III chassis, to be shared equally by Southern and Western National, were sent to Strachans to be bodied to the basic 35-seat Tilling design. Whilst the six allotted to SNOC were based initially at Seaton, WNOC's were allocated to Totnes, where Nos 1066 and 1071 (JUO 957/62) are pictured in the yard, frustratingly close to the Waterman's Arms public house. *Peter Yeomans*

In 1948/9, by which time its subsidiary companies were at last receiving sufficient numbers of new vehicles to meet an all-time record demand for travel by bus, the Tilling Association agreed to help out London Transport, then suffering its own vehicle shortage. Among others, Western National loaned 21 Bristol K/ECW double-deckers (and SNOC eight) straight from the manufacturers. Here Leyton-based No 887 (HOD 14), bound for Chingford, has a London Transport STL-class AEC Regent for company. *Ian Allan Library*

In March 1950 Stanley Kennedy, Chairman of the Tilling Group's Management Board, wrote to the British Transport Commission recommending that the operations and assets of the Western National and the newly nationalised Red & White companies in the Stroud area be transferred to the Bristol Tramways & Carriage Co Ltd. Well, there was no arguing with that. Western National's business at Stroud was handed over on 21 May 1950 at a book value of £77,245 (later amended to £61,255); the Bristol company was to take up a £450 annual tenancy of the property in London Road, Stroud, which remained in Western National ownership. There was little other consolation, save in one service between Stroud and Trowbridge, which for the time being Western National was permitted to retain. In contrast, in return for the transfer to the Bristol company of its own Stroud depot, Red & White received the former's Coleford depot and services operated in the Forest of Dean. However, Western National's London Road premises were eventually transferred to the Bristol Tramways & Carriage Co Ltd at a book value of £16,010 in September 1954. Although Stanley

Kennedy had further recommended that Western National's Trowbridge operations be transferred to the Bristol company, that was not in the event implemented at that time.

A noteworthy WNOC acquisition in February 1952 was the four stage-carriage services and excursions and tours from Quantock Hauliers Ltd, based at Watchet, Somerset. Services to Taunton from Bagborough, West Fitzhead and Cothelstone and another from Watchet to Bridgwater were numbered 417-20 in the WNOC series, and a garage in Bagborough became WNOC property, as did five Bedford and two Seddon single-deck buses and two Bedford and three Dennis Lancet coaches, these being numbered 3791-5, 3801/2, 3796/7 and 3798-800 respectively in the Western National fleet. Licences, property and vehicles involved cost WNOC £21,317.

In September 1950 WNOC had purchased a site in Plymouth Road, Tavistock, for £10,500 and laid plans for the erection of a garage thereon. This took rather longer than expected to bring to fruition, the contract for its construction — with J. Curswill & Sons Ltd — not being signed until June 1955. The building of a bus station in Tower Street, Taunton, had been a less troublesome project, and the tender of £23,041 from F. & E. Small was duly accepted in February 1951. In that month also WNOC had learned that its finally agreed restitution for damage from enemy action (via the Post War Refund scheme) was to be £105,460 3s 11d. Later that year an agreement with the Ministry of Supply resulted in WNOC's paying £3,000 for all of the buildings erected at the Laira Bridge site during 1942/3 (at the expense of the MoS) in connection with the Jeep-assembling Tilefer scheme. And in September 1951 WNOC at last agreed that a loan of £10,000, received as far back as 14 March 1942 from Southern National, should be repaid! The GWR versus the Southern Railway element was still alive and kicking.

*Above left and above:* In 1949 Western National invested in 15 examples (SNOC five) of Beadle's lightweight chassisless saloon, constructed entirely in its own workshops at Dartford, Kent. WNOC's first had a Sentinel engine, to be followed by 12 powered by Bedford and two by Morris. No 2015 (HOD 66) was a 35-seat Bedford-powered example. The characteristic 'bleary-eyed' rear-window shape of Beadle's coaches and saloon buses was carried to its structural limit in the design of this fascinating vehicle. *Colin Morris (both)*

*Above:* Taunton was a depot which prided itself in its capacity to cope with the maintenance of unusual vehicles and power units. Accordingly both Morris-engined variants of the chassisless Beadle saloons delivered to Western National, Nos 2019/20 (LTA 148/9) saw service there. Several Tilling Group companies seem to have received just a brace of the Beadle-Morris combination, Hants & Dorset being another example. *Peter Yeomans*

*Right:* Parked in the yard at Bridgwater, Somerset, are two vehicles rebodied in 1949 with Strachans' version of the standard 35-seat Tilling saloon body — Nos 3146 (VF 7645) and 3151 (VF 7661). Leyland Tiger TS3 models dating from 1930, both were originally coaches with United Automobile Services but were purchased from Eastern Counties in 1945 — and fitted with Gardner diesel engines in 1951. Also visible here are AEC Regent/ Beadle 52-seater No 4708 (YD 4708) and Bristol H5G/ECW 32-seater No 158 (OD 7843). *Alan Lambert collection*

*Right:* Western National's first Bristol H saloon, No 100 (FJ 8930) of 1933, was twice refurbished. Originally a Bristol-bodied 32-seater, it was altered (by the same firm) in 1940 to seat 35 passengers and then, in 1950, rebodied by Beadle with this Tilling-standard saloon design, produced under licence by several coachbuilders over a number of years.
The original Bristol radiator was considered sufficiently modern to warrant retention. *B. A. Jenkins*

*Left:* The first edition of Ian Allan's *Buses Illustrated* featured upon its cover a Hants & Dorset Bristol K. Issue No 4, dated April 1950 and costing 1s 6d (just 7½p), depicted a fine two-year-old coach, Western National Bedford OB/Duple 27-seater No 542 (HUO 695), on one of the well-patronised tours of the period. This now classic photograph was taken as the vehicle cruised westward over the Dart bridge at Holne, beneath Ryders Hill on Dartmoor Forest. *Colin Morris collection*

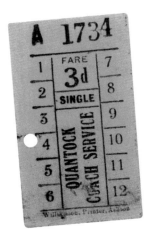

*Left:* In 1950 the Tilling Group Management Board convinced the British Transport Commission that Western National should be divested of its long-besieged depot at Stroud, Gloucestershire, and that this should be allotted at last to the Bristol Tramways & Carriage Co. This achieved, in May of that year, the Bristol company's priorities seem odd: rather than overpainting the Western National fleetname on the vehicles transferred it simply renumbered them into its own series. By the time this photograph was taken WNOC Bristol H No 129 (FJ 8959) had become BTCC No 2490 but still displayed 'Western National' in the destination box. *Andrew Waller collection*

In the early 1950s goods vehicles of Seddon manufacture were commonplace upon the roads of Britain. Less conspicuous was the passenger-carrying Seddon Mk IV. The versatile mechanics at Taunton took it in their stride when two Plaxton-bodied examples, Nos 3801/2 (KYC 292, 742) joined the Western National fleet in 1952 — along with 10 other single-deck vehicles — from local operator Quantock Hauliers Ltd, of Watchet. *Peter Yeomans*

Also among the vehicles taken over with Quantock Hauliers were three Dennis Lancet coaches with extremely handsome 35-seat bodywork by Duple of Hendon. Retained to continue the tours business established by Quantock's R. J. Street at Bagborough and Watchet — and that of WNOC at Taunton — was No 3798 (KYC 745). *Peter Yeomans*

The early 1950s was a most interesting period in terms of the variety of vehicle types to be found in service. Besides the latest deliveries were to be seen such surviving gems as this 1936 Dennis Mace with 25-seat Bristol bodywork, No 636 (CTA 529). In addition to the usual instruction to passengers to 'Wait until the bus stops' is a notice asking them to wait until the driver or conductor opens that sliding door. *Alan B. Cross*

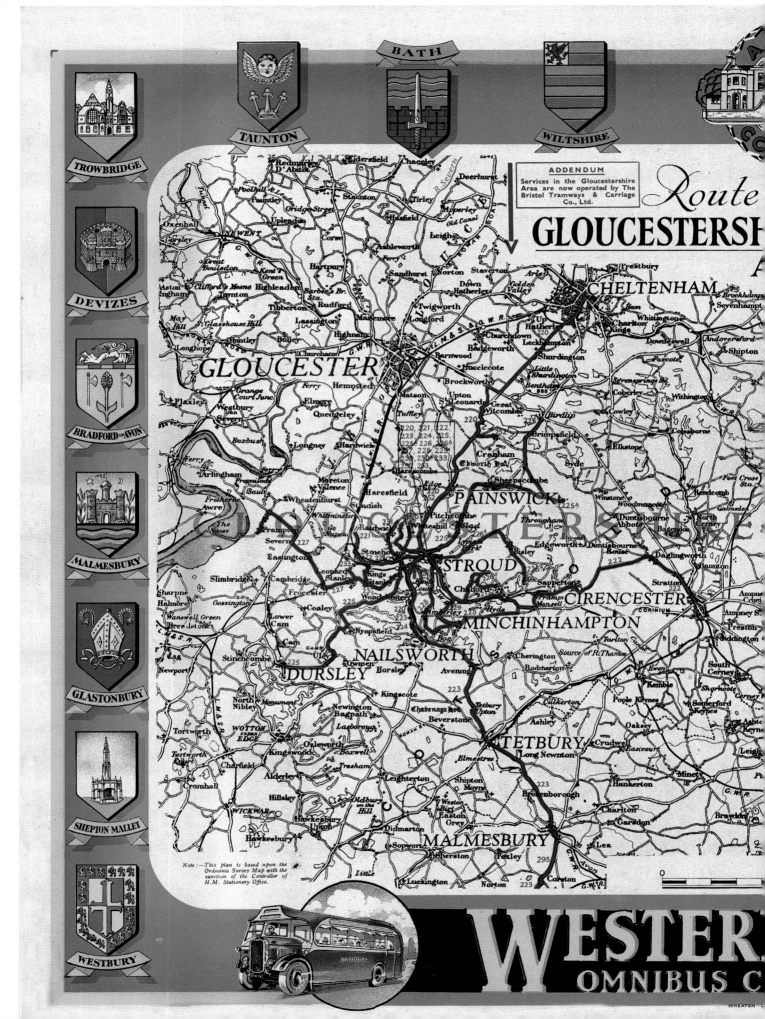

Map of
E & WILTSHIRE
A

**SOMERSET** · **GLOUCESTER** · **CHIPPENHAM** · **CHELTENHAM** · **WARMINSTER** · **CALNE** · **TETBURY** · **DORCHESTER** · **SHERBORNE** · **YEOVIL**

Routes operated by
ROYAL BLUE - GREYHOUND EXPRESS SERVICES

223, 241.   Service Numbers of Omnibus Routes.

Routes operated by
THE WESTERN NATIONAL OMNIBUS Cº LTD

10 MILES

NATIONAL
PANY LIMITED

During the 1950s Eastern Coach Works undertook an extensive programme of rebodying earlier Bristol vehicles with the same Series 2 style of bodywork introduced post World War 2; at the same time the low-line PV2 radiator replaced the earlier version. No 316 (DOD 505), a Bristol K5G/ECW lowbridge double-decker of 1940, was refitted thus in 1954 and is pictured working the short journey from Paignton to Stoke Gabriel. *Peter Yeomans*

The 'four river' route from Plymouth to Bigbury-on-Sea crossed the Rivers Plym, Yealm and Erme and came to a halt beside the estuary of the (Devon) Avon. No 283 (DDV 17) exemplifies the 20-year service life by now regularly achieved by WNOC vehicles. A Bristol K5G of 1939, only the driver's cab resembling its original Beadle bodywork, it had been rebuilt in ECW style by the same firm in 1950, to serve a further nine years. *Geoff Rixon*

On 30 November 1952 at the age of 71, Roland Buszard retired from WNOC/SNOC after 41 years' service, which had commenced with the National Steam Car Co Ltd. This coincided with the appointment as Chief Traffic Manager of Eric Horobin, returned from semi-military service in West Germany. The following month WNOC purchased for £5,000 a long-established firm with a very long name — The Porlock Weir, Porlock & Minehead Motor Service Co Ltd, trading as Blue Motors. That brought into the WNOC fleet two more vehicles: Nos 3819, an AEC Regal III, and 3820, a Dennis Lancet. A Bedford OB/Thurgood coach (3824) was added later, when Banfil & Barrington's Selene Coaches, of Mawnan Smith, Falmouth, was acquired.

On 17 February 1955 Claude Pickett was appointed a director to replace Major F. J. Chapple. Pickett became a member of the Plymouth Joint Services Committee just in time to take part in a disagreement over a proposed new bus station, and whether — as the company wished — WNOC vehicles should be permitted to continue using roadside stands as their termini in the city. WNOC (and SNOC) Chairman George Cardwell resigned that month, to be replaced by an odd choice (bearing in mind that it was he who had proposed the divesting of WNOC's Stroud depot, and Trowbridge as well, if he'd had his way) — that of Stanley Kennedy. But then the chairmen of subsidiary companies had long been chosen from above. Kennedy's mission was to lead another effort to amalgamate the Western and Southern National companies. This attempt at further 'moving and shaking' in that direction was of course approved

by the BTC but was nipped in the bud by none other than the Minister of Transport. Kennedy resigned in June 1957, to be replaced as Chairman by Claude Pickett.

A workaholic if ever there was one, Bernard Venn Smith, Director and General Manager, died at his desk on 28 September 1957. After an appropriate stasis of two months, Thomas W. H. Gailey replaced him in both posts.

The extensive scheme to remodel completely the war-torn centre of Plymouth, largely finished by 1958, included the construction of Breton Side bus station. As far as stage-carriage services were concerned this was to be operated jointly, the costs being shared on the PJS basis of 80% by the Corporation and 20% WNOC.

Inspired by Devon General's reintroduction of open-top double-deckers for summer seaside work at Torquay, WNOC and SNOC each purchased a couple of ex-Bristol Omnibus Co K5Gs to be cut down for similar purpose. Western National's pair were sent to work at Falmouth, principally between the town centre and Gyllyngvase Beach on service 159, being employed thus between 1958 and 1964. Pictured in 'reversed' livery is No 3823 (FHT 106). *Alan Lambert*

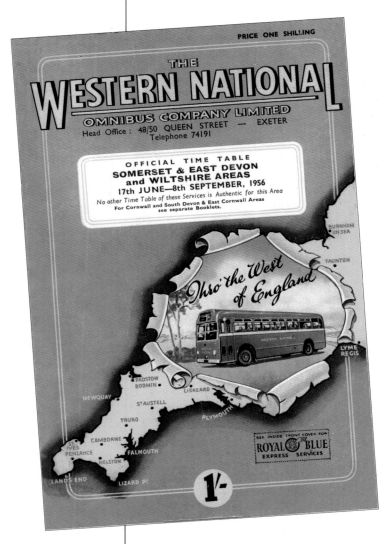

Following the after-effects of the Finance Act 1950 and throughout the next decade the cost of Bristol/ECW vehicles rose considerably year by year. In 1951 a double-decker had cost £3,300, a single-decker £3,000, and a coach £4,000. When the time came to place the order for the 1957 programme, the comparative costs were £4,750, £4,350 and £4,950 respectively — enough to signify that the zenith of post World War 2 profitability had passed.

As though in response to Stanley Kennedy's efforts, on 15 June 1960 the development of a site at the Conigre, Trowbridge, for a bus station and garage was approved at an estimated cost of £25,000. It was to cost a bit more than that: the following year the tender of Bicknell & Sons of Bristol was accepted for its construction at £40,476. Costs generally continued to rise sharply: by June 1959 work upon replacement head offices on the existing site in Queen Street, Exeter, was underway, the main contract having been awarded to John Garrett & Sons Ltd of Plymouth at £131,661. The project to provide a bus station in Paignton (jointly with Devon General) was also well on its way to fruition. (See *Glory Days: Devon General*.)

In January 1959 WNOC had purchased the goodwill of Heybrook Bay Motor Services Ltd of Down Thomas, Plymouth, together with its technical ownership of Coombes (Plymouth) Ltd, for a total of £11,500. Heybrook Bay had provided services which were merged into the PJS arrangement within the city as routes 54 and 55.

December 1959 saw Thomas Gailey appointed a member of the Tilling Group Management Board. He retained his WNOC directorship but was replaced as General Manager by Henry L. Ellis with effect from 1 January 1960 — the year in which Roger Wigmore was appointed joint Secretary.

As the 1960s commenced there was considerable movement in the WNOC property market, with

COACH GUIDE CORNWALL

WESTERN · NATIONAL
OMNIBUS · COMPANY · LIMITED
IN ASSOCIATION WITH BRITISH RAILWAYS
PRICE 6d

the first indications of downscaling — set to gain momentum as the decade advanced. First, with the new premises at the Conigre, Trowbridge, coming into use, the former garage in Bythesea Road was sold for £9,200. At Minehead it took intervention from the Minister of Transport to overcome the local authority's objection to the development of a bus station and enlargement of the garage. Plans for a bus station at East Quay, Bridgwater, and for another at Union Street, Camborne, went ahead, as did those for extensions at Falmouth and at Callington. On the other hand, garages at Bagborough (Somerset) and Kuggar (Cornwall) were sold off.

In 1964 Claude Pickett was replaced as Chairman by Thomas W. H. Gailey, who was to serve in that role for four years until in turn being succeeded by J. T. E. Robinson. In 1967 Brian T. Hancock replaced George J. Brown as Chief Engineer, and Leslie T. Duncan was appointed Traffic Manager.

On the vehicle front, 1963 witnessed some most unusual additions to WNOC's coach fleet in the form of six Leylands — one Royal Tiger (No 3800) and five Tiger Cubs (3801-5) — and one Harrington Contender integral (3806) transferred from Silver Star of Porton Down, after that firm had been purchased by Wilts & Dorset Motor Services Ltd. In 1965 eight Bristol LS coaches (Nos 3807-14) acquired second-hand from Eastern National continued the numerical series and added interest to the decade's standard intake of FLF, RELH, MW and SUL models. Pending the arrival of a replacement for the Bristol SUL, now at the end of its production run, WNOC was obliged in 1966 to look elsewhere for a vehicle of similar seating capacity, the radical choice being Bedford's VAM5. Twelve such chassis were sent to ECW, which held things up somewhat by adapting MW body frames to complete the task. The following year new FLFs earmarked for WNOC were sent to the Bristol Omnibus Co Ltd (as it now called itself), which needed their extra capacity in exchange for 12 60-seat Bristol FSFs dating from 1961. In 1968 the first examples of the preferred Bristol LH

41-seat saloon were delivered to depots in Cornwall. The same year saw the opening of two new bus stations of note — one at Earle Street in Yeovil (which SNOC was to use initially), the other on the Albert Quay site in Penzance. At national (with a lower-case 'n'!) level politics were set once again to bring about change in the operating industry. The THC's days were numbered.

In 1960 WNOC took delivery of nine Bristol SUS4A/ECW 30-seat buses, the SUS being the short version of Bristol's SU lightweight underfloor-engined saloon. All were fitted with Albion four-cylinder engines, and they proved most suitable for the narrow lanes of Cornwall, in particular. Here No 602 (674 COD) eases itself down to the seafront at Mousehole, where once lived Dolly Pentreath, the last person to speak the Cornish language. *Mike Stephens*

*Above:* The lady demonstrates an air of desperation — or disbelief — that this Bristol LWL/ECW 39-seat saloon will actually set out for its stated destination of Penzance railway station from WNOC's otherwise deserted outstation at Land's End. Built in 1952, No 1647 (LTA 845) had another three years' service ahead of it when photographed on 30 July 1965. *Mike Stephens*

*Upper right:* Parked beside the Talavera Hotel at Newquay bus station on 1 August 1965 was Bristol LWL6B/ECW 39-seater saloon No 1630 (LTA 789), delivered to Western National in 1951. Pictured awaiting its next journey to St Austell via St Dennis on route 58A, it would be withdrawn the year after the taking of this fine photograph. *Mike Stephens*

*Right:* Another full day of glorious summer seems in prospect as, with St Michael's Mount as a distant backdrop, Bristol SUS4A/ECW 30-seater No 603 (675 COD) of 1960, awaits custom for a trip to Mousehole via Newlyn Bridge on service 9. *Mike Stephens*

*Above:* It is easy to forget how diminutive was Bristol's K-type double-decker, compared with today's equivalents. Here Western National 966 (KUO 979), a K5G/ECW 55-seat lowbridge model delivered to Southern National in 1949 and transferred in June 1963, stands in Camborne bus station in August 1965, having arrived from Helston. *Mike Stephens*

*Left:* Parked beside Western National's Camborne garage in August 1965 was three-year-old Bristol FLF6G/ECW 68-seater No 1990 (136 HUO), having lost two seats in 1963 in favour of extra luggage space. The overall greyness of the background reflects the presence locally of Cornwall's long-established mining industry. *Mike Stephens*

At rest in Newquay bus station in the mid-1960s are an interesting pair of Western National vehicles on tour duties. On the left is Bristol MW6G No 1392 (261 KTA), a 39-seater with stepped-waistline ECW coach bodywork, delivered in 1962. New the same year, Bristol SUL4A No 419 (269 KTA) was also bodied by ECW as a coach, with 33 seats, but had been downgraded to dual-purpose status in 1968. *Mike Stephens*

Parked beside the River Camel at Padstow, in north Cornwall — Southern National territory — is Bristol SUL4A/ECW 33-seat coach No 419 (269 KTA), delivered in 1962. Having been downgraded in 1968 it would be renumbered as 1219 in 1971, remaining in WNOC service for a further two years thereafter. *Mike Stephens*

Its destination screens set to read 'WESTERN TOUR', Bristol MW6G/ECW 39-seat coach No 1393 (262 KTA), one of the last coaches delivered in green and cream (in 1962) but destined to be a Royal Blue vehicle from 1970, stands in Newquay bus station in August 1965 beside a Bristol K6B retained for short journeys to St Dennis; at that time only single-deckers could get through to St Austell. *Mike Stephens*

Setting out on a tour from Newquay bus and coach station is one of a rather special batch of vehicles new in 1963. Bristol MW6G/ECW 39-seater No 1406 (744 MDV) was one of 14 of its type to be delivered in Royal Blue livery, rather than the cream and green used hitherto. For that first season they displayed Royal Blue fleetnames also but afterward bore the logo of the operating company. *Mike Stephens*

Working an extension to Penzance of service 21A from Falmouth, Bristol FLF/ECW 70-seater No 2072 (AUO 519B) awaits departure time beside the Angel Hotel in Coinagehall Street, Helston. As befits a trip along the shore of Mounts Bay beneath a cloudless sky, the upper deck is already comfortably filled. The bus was new in 1964. *Mike Stephens*

Lodekka line-up at Penzance railway station, 1960s-style. From left to right are LD6B No 1870 (OTT 9) of 1954 and FLF6Bs 2096 (BOD 38C) of 1965 and 2067 (AUO 514B) of 1964. Just visible in the background is an independent operator's vehicle providing a link to the Heliport. *Mike Stephens*

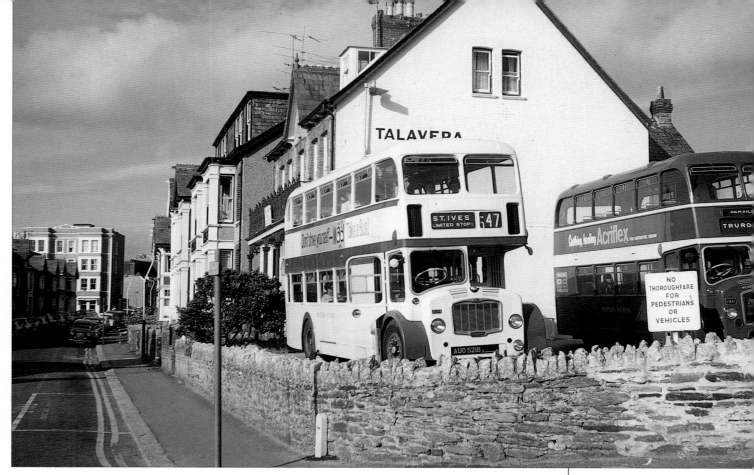

The driver's door has been left a-swinging on No 2074 (AUO 521B), a Bristol FLF/ECW 70-seater new in 1964. Photographed at Newquay in August 1969, it had been painted three years previously in a reversed livery for use on the limited-stop service to St Ives, for many years route 37 but recently renumbered 547. No 2074 would revert to standard (albeit NBC) livery in 1977. *Mike Stephens*

Bristol FLF6B/ECW 70-seater No 2044 (ATA 125B) of 1964 was another of the trio repainted in a reversed livery for operation on the Newquay–St Ives express service — a colour scheme which served to accentuate its Cave-Browne-Cave air intakes. However, it was discovered in 1969 on route 562 overlooking Carrick Roads, one of the finest harbours in the country. *Mike Stephens*

At the head of the line-up at Paris Street, Exeter, in August 1966 is Western National No 3802 (KMW 644), painted in Royal Blue livery and ready to work a relief journey on the express service to Plymouth. This vehicle was one of seven passed on to WNOC by Wilts & Dorset Motor Services after the latter had taken over Silver Star, of Porton Down, in 1963. This one, a Leyland Tiger Cub PSUC1/2, carried 41-seat Harrington coachwork. *Mike Stephens*

All the Royal Blue coaches having departed, a Western National Bristol MW6G/ECW 39-seat coach — in immaculate condition — looms large in Exeter coach station. No 1397 (266 KTA) and its distant companions remain at rest, having served in a familiar role as weekend relief vehicles on Royal Blue services to various locations but principally on journeys to/from London Victoria. *Mike Stephens*

A late-1960s view of the smart end of Newquay bus station — that devoted to Royal Blue express services, as well as private hires and tours. Into the latter category, on one of those cloudless days that Cornwall frequently enjoys, fits Bristol SUL4A/ECW 33-seat coach No 419 (269 KTA) as it occupies the 'next departure' bay. *Mike Stephens*

Photographed in August 1968, Bristol SUL4A No 421 (271 KTA) was originally a 33-seat ECW-bodied coach but had recently been converted to dual-purpose OMO configuration. On Royal Blue relief service from Dartmouth, it is pictured approaching Exeter coach station. Beyond the roundabout in Heavitree Road is the City of Exeter bus (originally tram) depot. *Mike Stephens*

Probably with a sigh of relief from the ECW workforce, Western National's No 705 (KDV 135F) has been parked outside the 'Coach Factory' at Lowestoft prior to delivery. One of a dozen Bedford VAM5 chassis sent there to receive 41-seat bus bodywork, it had taken considerably longer than expected to complete, because of the time spent in adapting ECW's standard body frames to a non-Bristol chassis. The batch entered service in the latter half of 1967. *Mike Stephens*

Serving upon an ex-GWR Road Motor Department route from Plymouth to Dartmouth in October 1969 is a vehicle which, together with its fellows, took so long to construct that its original role of stopgap was not fulfilled; they were however, much liked by those who drove or rode upon them. One of 12 Bedford VAM/ECW 41-seaters delivered in 1967, No 702 (KDV 132F) was photographed at Torcross. *R. J. Crawley*

# NBC's Western National

In 1969 Western National took delivery of its first Bristol VRT rear-engined double-deckers. Seating 70 passengers apiece, the 10 vehicles featured the flat-windscreen design of contemporary ECW bodywork. Ideal for urban work, No 1059 (OTA 293G) was sent new to Plymouth, there to operate on Joint Services routes. *D. Withers*

PRIME MINISTER Harold Wilson was said to have considered Edward Heath's Conservative Government (1970-4) but a slight bout of hiccups in the midst of his Labour administration (1964-70/4-6). One of the major pieces of legislation slotted into Wilson's first period in office had been the Transport Act 1968. Among other things this had sought to push the political 'swingometer' back to the left and repair the 'damage' done to the British Transport Commission in 1962 when it had been undone by Harold MacMillan's Conservatives and replaced by the Transport Holding Company, intended by the Tories as a temporary measure pending a return to private ownership.

The THC in turn was now supplanted by the National Bus Company — and this 'National' meant that it was the property of the nation; to the question of why, therefore, NBC was designated a 'Company' it has thus far proved impossible to find a satisfactory explanation! Nevertheless, with effect from 1 January 1969 all 42 of the nationalised territorial bus companies became subsidiaries of the National Bus Company, and each was obliged to seek the approval of that body before carrying out any radical changes, just as had been the case in BTC days. In the event, most such changes would be imposed by NBC in the first place.

Some 12 months of discussion thereafter brought to an end Western National's control of the services based upon Trowbridge and Chippenham and their transfer — with effect from 1 January 1970 — to the Bristol Omnibus Co Ltd, which purchased from Western National for £34,844 the garage and vehicle park at The Conigre, Trowbridge.

During the same period the oft-discussed 'amalgamation' of Southern National and Western National was at last effected by applying to the Traffic Commissioners for the transfer of all the road-traffic licences held by the Southern company to the Western National Omnibus Co Ltd. The assets and liabilities of Southern National as at 31 December 1968 were formally made over to Western National for a consideration of £1,026,599. On 8 January 1970 all the freehold properties of Southern National were conveyed at book value to Western National. The British Railways (Southern Region) representatives were no longer in a position to complain, even had they wished to do so. All the ex-Southern National properties and services were now set to be operated by the enlarged Western National Omnibus Co Ltd, save where diminishing traffic or vigorous competition from independent operators was likely to make such activity unprofitable.

The National Bus Company was, from its inception, not favourably disposed to competing with those independents when it came to the provision of private hires, excursions and tours. Before December 1969 was out Western National had begun its withdrawal from such work with the sale of its excursions and tours at Yeovil to Darch & Willcox for £400 and those at Chard to Bristol-based Wessex Coaches Ltd for a mere £100. The following June a rather more respectable figure of £1,200 was paid by A. Walker & Son for the goodwill of similar work from Taunton and Wiveliscombe. As 1970 drew to a close, tours from Perranporth passed to S. R. Mitchell & Son for a similar sum, while those at Mevagissey were bought by B. Ede for £500. Visitors to the West Country were in any case now using their own cars and towed caravans in increasing numbers.

A Bristol LD6G Lodekka with 60-seat Eastern Coach Works body, No 1951 (503 BTA) was one of a batch of 17 identical vehicles delivered to Western National in 1959. Photographed, shortly after a repaint, at Plymouth's Breton Side bus station in May 1972, it is set to make a journey across the Tamar Bridge on a short 'two counties' run to Forder, in Cornwall. *Mike J. Stephens*

Nicely lit at WNOC's Ticklemore Street garage in Totnes are Bristol SUL4A/ECW 36-seat saloon No 686 (EDV 541D), having worked in on service 164 from Halwell, and FLF6G/ECW 68-seater No 2019 (824 KDV), with blind set for a short working to Paignton of route 127. The photograph dates from May 1972. *Mike Stephens*

Land and buildings joined the 'For Sale' list also. Heading the exodus was the Trelawny garage, Penzance, shortly followed by 4 Marine Crescent, Seaton, whilst the garage in South Street, Taunton, was purchased for a goodly sum by White Bros (Taunton) Ltd. The garage at Marlborough Road, Ilfracombe, was put on the market, the land (leased from British Rail) adjoining Barnstaple Town station was surrendered, and negotiations commenced with Hants & Dorset Motor Services Ltd for the transfer to that company of the Swanage depot, although these went on a little longer than expected. These premises, at 66 Kings Road West — together with six vehicles — eventually passed to H&D on 1 January 1974, for £6,626, Western National retreating west of Lulworth Cove.

The 'new vehicle' requirement for 1972 saw 13 Leyland National saloons, 12 Bristol LH saloons and six Bristol RELH coaches deleted from the programme. This was balanced somewhat by the news that NBC had 'approved' the transfer to Western National, with effect from 1 January 1971 at net book value, of the assets and liabilities of the Devon General Omnibus & Touring Co Ltd. (See *Glory Days: Devon General*.) These included the Devon General fleet and premises, its staff being offered employment with Western National on conditions no less favourable than they already enjoyed. In addition an assignment from Devon General was made for the lease of Exeter Bus & Coach Station, together with the tenancy of the ex-Corporation garage in Heavitree Road, Exeter.

Framed by a pair of Plymouth City Transport Leyland Atlanteans, a 1965 Bristol FLF/ECW heads along Royal Parade on Joint Services route 5 (Elburton–City Centre–Torpoint Ferry). Recorded in May 1972, the scene reflects the 1950s reconstruction and remodelling of the city centre following the devastating air raids suffered by Plymouth during World War 2. (Compare with wartime picture of the Bristol saloon, also bound for Torpoint Ferry, on page 46.) *Mike Stephens*

Pictured at Totnes Market Square in May 1972 with blinds set for Harbertonford (one of those longish joined-up names prevalent in south Devon), Bristol SUL4A/ECW dual-purpose 33-seater No 1222 (272 KTA) was originally a coach, numbered 422. Equipped for stage-carriage work in 1967, it was renumbered in 1971. *Mike Stephens*

A 'period piece' collection of Bristol/ECW saloons at Torpoint depot in May 1972. From left are LH6L No 751 (POD 810H), its stated destination of Cremyll recalling the Millbrook ferry service, similar No 752 (POD 811H), MW6G No 1798 (VDV 767), lately on a Plymouth-area private-hire duty, and LH6L No 750 (POD 809H), last used on service 86 from Cremyll. The depot premises, in Trevol Road, were inherited from NO&T, which had acquired them from Devon Motor Transport in 1928.
*Mike J. Stephens*

As vehicles more suited to express work became available, so those of the SU type delivered as coaches were downgraded to dual-purpose status. An SUL4A/ECW 33-seater new in 1961, 415 (920 GUO) was so modified in 1968, being renumbered three years later as 1215, in which guise it is pictured in Truro in 1975. *Mike Stephens*

Four days later, the Western Area Traffic Commissioners having granted the necessary road-service licence, Western National introduced a stage-carriage service between Taunton and Minehead, following withdrawal of the rail service between those towns. However, when, at the end of 1971, it became necessary for Western National to provide a replacement for the rail service on the now-closed Exeter–Okehampton line it dealt with the matter in radical fashion. Rather than operate its own vehicles it paid W. J. O. Jennings Ltd (£1,900 per annum), and Phillips & Co (£600pa), to run the service for a period of two years from the closure of the line — a cost-cutting move of which the late Sir Frederick Heaton would most surely have approved. Three months earlier Jennings had acquired Western National's garage in Lansdown Road, Bude.

The sale of premises continued apace, the list including the famous Blackboy Road garage, Exeter, the Station Hall at Westward Ho! and garages at Lynton (Lee Road), Moretonhampstead (Court Street), Delabole (High Street), St Just, Tiverton (Old Road) and Penzance (Rack Park, Morrab Road) as well as offices, cottages and land at Helston. In their stead came a marked increase in the use of rented accommodation.

The National Bus Company itself found it necessary to rationalise, its original 'operational areas' — 10 of them nationwide — quickly being reduced to six. In short order, with effect from 1 April 1972, the number was down to just three. The newly created Southern Area was divided into three, and selected general managers were elevated to the rank of Chief General Manager. Appointed thus in the West Country was E. W. A. Butcher, a Western National director between 1 September 1970 and 31 December 1973. As elsewhere, the axe fell unceremoniously upon Western National's serving officers, in particular Henry Leslie Ellis, with the company since 1942 progressively as Secretary, General Manager and director; R. J. Ellery was obliged to resign as a director, as was John Palette, a director since 1969. The biggest scalp, however, was that of J. T. E. Robinson, Chairman of the Board since December 1968.

Replacement directors were David S. Deacon, a director from April 1972, and Ian Campbell, a director and General Manager with effect from 1 May 1972. Notable survivors were Frank Pointon, a director since January 1971, Traffic Manager Leslie T. Duncan and Company Secretary Roger Wigmore. In the boardroom the concept of 'Chairman' faded from use, and a senior director was declared to be 'in the chair' (as directed generally by NBC) for each meeting, which by 21 October 1975 had reached No 214. After that no-one seemed to bother with such historical niceties — and someone would appear to have lost count earlier on anyhow. Meanwhile, in typical NBC style, such meetings were as likely to be held in Hove, Reading or Bristol as in Queen Street, Exeter.

During the early 1970s Western National's representation upon the Plymouth Joint Committee comprised E. W. A. Butcher, Ian Campbell and L. T. Duncan, the last being replaced as Traffic Manager in 1975 by Michael Rourke, ex-Traffic Manager of Southdown — an example of the placement by NBC in what had been Tilling-oriented subsidiaries of officers whose careers had

*Above:* In Kimberley Road, Falmouth — a pleasantly leafy setting — No 676 (EDV 531D) was caught on camera running on service 564 to Helford Passage, on that most beautiful eponymous river. New in 1966, the bus is a Bristol SUL4A with 36-seat ECW bodywork — a type eventually supplanted on the production line by the Bristol LH. *Mike Stephens*

*Above right:* Beneath overcast skies, Bristol LH6L/ECW 41-seater No 715 (MUO 327F) of 1968 sets off from Penzance for service on a variation of route 512 to Madron — a journey of just 1¾ miles. In common with others of its batch this vehicle would later be rebuilt with deeper windscreen and revised destination display. *Mike Stephens*

*Above:* Having taken over Southern National's Bideford works as an emergency measure during World War 2, Western National returned in force beside the River Torridge in 1970. Delivered to WNOC in 1971, Bristol RELL6G/ECW 53-seat saloon No 2754 (UTT 557J) was photographed in 1982 running light on Bideford Quayside, where in years gone by Southern National buses paused in one long line. *G. B. Wise*

previously progressed in British Electric Traction's territorial bus companies.

In March 1974, seeking to move with the times by computerising its records, Western National combined forces with Hants & Dorset and Bristol Omnibus to use a regional computer recently installed at the latter's headquarters — a further nod in the direction of a company Western National once controlled. On file that year was a slight reversal of NBC's nationwide trend, for when Western National obtained a licence from West Dorset District Council for the use of that authority's bus/coach station at Bridport, it took the opportunity to purchase (for £350) from Wessex Coaches (Bristol) Ltd the latter's excursions licence from that town. Later in the year Wessex would sell much of the remainder of its business to NBC, this being included within the newly formed National Travel (South West), but presumably it made sense for excursions from a small town some distance from Bristol to be run by the local bus-operating subsidiary.

*Left:* Among the varied fleet that became Western National's responsibility after the takeover of Devon General were the latter's famous 'Sea Dogs' — nine early Leyland Atlanteans with convertible-open-top Metro-Cammell bodywork. Named after the most famous 'sea dog' of them all, No 926 (926 GTA) *Sir Francis Drake* later received Western National fleetnames for use at Falmouth but retained a basically red livery. *Martin Curtis*

*Below left:* In 1972 five more Atlanteans, with Alexander bodywork — which always looked a little odd in Western National livery — joined the fleet. Although less than a year old, they were transferred from Western Welsh in April of that year. All five were sent to work from Callington. No 1020 (VUH 377J), the first of the batch, was photographed at Plymouth in June 1972. *G. F. Walker*

*Above right:* I. K. Brunel's impressive railway bridge, carrying the Great Western main line across the river separating Devon from Cornwall, is nowadays dwarfed by the Tamar road bridge (opened in October 1961), the latter permitting the revision of numerous bus routes into and out of Plymouth from the west. Against this dramatic and historical backdrop No 1022 (VUH 379J), an ex-Western Welsh Leyland Atlantean PDR1/3 with 73-seat Alexander bodywork, heads southward into Plymouth in September 1975. *Mike Stephens*

*Left:* One of 12 delivered to WNOC in early 1972 (six of which were allocated to the red 'Devon General' fleet), No 1255 (VOD 125K) was a Bristol LHS6L — the short version of the LH — with 33-seat Marshall bodywork. It was photographed in the early 1980s working a town service in Bodmin. *Chris Drew*

*Below left:* The full-size version of the Bristol LH/ECW combination seated 43 passengers and accounted for the vast majority of the type's production run. WNOC No 1589 (NFJ 589M) was delivered in 1973 and allocated to Plymouth depot. When photographed in October 1982 it was operating between the city centre and the shore base at HMS *Raleigh* via Torpoint Ferry, on a service that would later be worked by dedicated Leyland Nationals. *M. Fowler*

Leaving Penzance bus station for St Erth and St Ives in 1975 is Bristol LD6G/ECW 60-seater No 1939 (VDV 756). Delivered to Western National in 1958, by the time this photograph was taken it had but one more year to serve before retirement, its still-smart appearance testimony to the standards maintained at WNOC. *Mike Stephens*

*En route* from Newquay to St Ives on what used to be route 37 but has by now become the 547, No 2074 (AUO 521B), a Bristol FLF6G/ECW 70-seater of 1964, departs Camborne bus station in 1975. This vehicle was one of three of its type repainted in reversed livery in 1966 specifically for use on express journeys on this service. By 1973 an NBC version of this colour scheme had been applied to all three vehicles. *Mike Stephens*

Having travelled north-west from Falmouth, No 1997 (802 KDV), a 1962-vintage Bristol FLF6B/ECW 70-seater, negotiates the mildly spectacular approach to Truro bus station. Photographed in 1975, the bus still sports a white steering wheel, fitted when new to remind drivers of its 8ft width. *Mike Stephens*

Departing Plymouth's Breton Side bus station in bright sunshine, Bristol FLF6G/ECW 70-seater No 2113 (EDV 525D), with Cave-Browne-Cave heating equipment — disclosed by the air intakes on either side of the destination display — shows off its lengthy lines. Delivered in 1966, it was photographed in 1975 *en route* for Tavistock. *Mike Stephens*

Bristol FLF6G/ECW 70-seater No 2093 (BOD 35C) approaches Truro bus station, having travelled up from Penzance on what used to be WNOC route 18. In the background, at 'The Green', is the bus station used by local independent operators. *Mike Stephens*

The 1970s was very much a time for drawing in the horns, and numerous second-hand vehicles joined the fleet, from Bristol Omnibus, Mansfield District, Southdown, Trent, Gosport & Fareham, Hants & Dorset, Midland Red and Maidstone & District. From the last-named came No 1000 (580 RKJ), a Metro-Cammell-bodied Leyland Atlantean PDR1/1 acquired in 1975 and allocated to Helston depot. *R. M. Tulloch*

From east to west! Enjoying a change of scenery, perhaps, is No 1043 (43 DKT), a Leyland Atlantean PDR1/1 with 71-seat lowbridge Weymann bodywork, transferred to WNOC in 1976 from Maidstone & District as one of no fewer than 28 Atlanteans acquired from that company. Photographed later that year, it was passing Fistral Bay while operating a local service from Newquay. *Mike Stephens*

The year 1975 saw an increase in the trend toward leasing rather than ownership. In addition to entering into an agreement with Plymouth Corporation for the use of an office at its Breton Side bus station (£625 per annum) and an office at 5 Exeter Street (£700pa) — as well as a considerably less expensive arrangement with South Hams District Council (£30pa) for the lease of its bus terminal at Kingsbridge — there commenced a similar policy in relation to the vehicles themselves. Whenever NBC required it to do so Western National and its fellow subsidiaries were obliged to sell to and lease back from nominated firms new buses allotted and delivered to them with effect from 1 November 1975. The scheme commenced with such an arrangement with Lloyds Leasing Ltd,

followed by others with Hambros Bank Ltd, Bus Manufacturers Ltd, Lombard North Central Leasing Ltd, Midland Montagu Leasing (UK) Ltd, Eastlease Ltd, Lazard Leasing Ltd, Williams & Glynn's Leasing Co Ltd and W & G Industrial Leasing Ltd. To give an idea of the sums of money involved in such transactions, the orders (placed in December 1975) for Western National's 1977 vehicle programme took into account the following specimen prices (always subject to rising costs, altered specifications, etc):

Bristol VRT/ECW 75-seat double-decker
  @ £20,900 each (£21,300 with removable roof)
Leyland National 52-seat saloon @ £19,700 each
Bristol LH/Plaxton 43-seat dual-purpose saloon
  @ £14,500 each
Leyland Leopard/Plaxton 51-seat coach
  @ £20,800 each

In the search for economies the 1977 programme was amended in December 1976, so that six Bristol LH/ECW single-deckers were substituted for six Leyland Nationals, 'showing an estimated reduction in the cost of the programme of £35,000' — which amount (if you care to work out the figures for individual vehicles) gives a clue as to how rapidly prices were rising at this time.

*Above:* Running light from Penzance bus station in August 1975 is No 2918 (60 GUO), a one-time Royal Blue coach new to Southern National in 1961 and transferred — like all the latter's vehicles — to WNOC in 1969. Originally numbered 2255, it was rebuilt as a bus in 1973, emerging in NBC green and white. *Mike Stephens*

*Right:* Among the stopgap acquisitions of the mid-1970s was Bristol MW6G/ECW 43-seater No 3009 (269 HNU), transferred in 1974 from Mansfield District. Still sporting additional chrome trim, befitting its role as a dual-purpose vehicle, it was photographed in Helston in September 1975. *Mike J. Stephens*

*Left:* With screen set for Newlyn Bridge and Mousehole — a charming little fishing port if ever there was one — on what used to be National's 262 (and after that WNOC's 9) route is Bristol LHS6L/Marshall 33-seater No 1253 (VOD 123K), starting off southward along the western side of Mounts Bay in 1975. *Mike Stephens*

*Left:* Competition at Penzance in 1975: emerging from the bus station on the Promenade is a neat little Albion Nimbus — a pretty rare bird in these parts — operated by Harvey, of Mousehole. Its registration a clue to its original owner, Halifax Corporation, RJX 250 would survive until Harvey sold out to WNOC. *Mike Stephens*

A rare type was the 30ft Bristol LDL6G/ECW, only seven of which were constructed. They included a pair of 70-seaters delivered to WNOC in 1957. Both were converted to open-top form in 1972/3, later being painted in NBC leaf green and white. Photographed at Penzance in 1975, No 1936 (VDV 753) was named *Sir Humphry Davy*; its twin, No 1935, was *Admiral Boscawen*. *Mike Stephens*

Waiting outside Redruth railway station, with a Leyland National for company, is Bristol FLF6G/ECW 70-seater No 1968 (467 FTT) — WNOC's first example of the FLF Lodekka variant, delivered in 1960. When photographed, in 1976, it was working service 546 to Illogan and Portreath. *Mike Stephens*

*Above:* Pictured in Falmouth in 1975 is Bristol RELL6G/ECW 53-seater No 2763 (ATA 763L), with blind set for a local journey from Falmouth Moor to Trelissick Road. The RE/ECW combination produced an elegant vehicle that was much preferred by operators to the Leyland National, which supplanted it. *Mike Stephens*

*Left:* No 1594 (NFJ 594M) was one of a batch of 12 Bristol LH6L/ECW 43-seaters delivered to Western National in 1973. Ten other LHs delivered the same year had 39-seat coach bodywork by Marshall for use on Royal Blue services. *Mike Stephens*

*Left:* Passing the Broadmead Hotel in Kimberley Park Road, Falmouth, is No 1600 (NFJ 600M), a Bristol LH6L/ECW 43-seater new in 1973 — at which time WNOC was making a concerted attempt to match fleet and registration numbers. Photographed in July 1976, it was operating on route 561 between Falmouth Moor and Mylor Bridge. *Mike Stephens*

*Above:* Pictured at Land's End, in the days before that location became a 'theme park' attracting many more coaches than can be seen in this photograph, is No 1076 (BFJ 176L), a Bristol VRTSL/ECW 75-seater of 1973, standing beside the 'dormy shed' (and herring gulls) before departing for Penzance on a one-time GWR bus route that later became WNOC's service 1. *Mike Stephens*

*Above:* On the last leg of its journey from Penzance to Land's End route 501 used to make a short diversion to Sennen Cove. Here, with Whitesand Bay forming a backdrop, Bristol VRT 1076 (BFJ 176L) passes Maria's Lane as it climbs back up to the A30 road. Like others of its batch reallocated to Penzance depot, this bus had earlier seen service at Torquay. *Mike Stephens*

*Left:* A pair of Western National vehicles dramatically lit against a backdrop of gathering storm clouds at Helston in July 1976. The newer of the two, turning into Monument Road from Coinagehall Street *en route* from Falmouth to Penzance on service 502, is Bristol VRT/ECW 75-seater No 1071 (BFJ 171L) of 1973. *Mike Stephens*

Making an empty after-service run along the seafront at Penzance is Bristol VRT/ECW 75-seater No 1079 (GTA 49N) of 1975. Although the bus was photographed in September of that year, its displayed advertisements suggest that it too had had a short spell at Torquay. *Mike Stephens*

Pictured in brand-new condition on service 590 from Truro (extended to Falmouth Docks) is Leyland National No 2803 (GFJ 667N) of 1975. Despite its smart appearance here this *magnum opus*, produced at NBC's bidding, was never a popular type nationwide with those who had to drive or maintain it. *Mike Stephens*

The transfer to Western National, with effect from 2 January 1971, of the operations and vehicles of its old rival, the Devon General Omnibus & Touring Co, saw the retention of many of the latter's recognisable characteristics. Among these was the basic hue of DG's rolling stock. As a case in point, No 926 (926 GTA) a Leyland Atlantean/Metro-Cammell 'Sea Dog' open-topper, saw continued service at Falmouth, running to Pendennis Point or Carrick Roads. *Mike Stephens*

A Bristol SUL4A with 36-seat ECW bus bodywork, No 658 (427 HDV) was new in 1962 to Southern National. After that company was subsumed under WNOC this vehicle, along with three others of its type, was repainted in NBC poppy red and white with Devon General fleetnames for use in DG territory. By now back at an original Western National garage, it is pictured in Camborne in July 1976, having arrived on route 545 from Townshend. *Mike Stephens*

In November 1976 Western National was antici-pating the transfer from Southdown Motor Services Ltd of two Ford-based Alexander midibuses 'at an estimated cost of £10,500 each subject to rise and fall [in value] and the availability of a Bus Grant'. Clearly, balancing the books was no job for the faint-hearted. Rumour has it that when Southdown had that brace of midibuses foisted upon it by NBC, no-one at Brighton had much idea as to what to use them for, and the company was doubtless only too pleased to send them west.

It was at this time (December 1976) that a proposal to dispense with Bridgwater bus station was upon the table 'if support from the local authority is not forthcoming'. It was agreed in principle to offer the property to NBC associate Omnibus Estates Ltd, but, in the event, NBC authorised its disposal for 'not less than £70,000'. Sedgemoor District Council found itself unable to finance the purchase at that time for continued use as a bus station, but in 1981 it was eventually sold at a price beyond the reserve. The sale of Totnes bus station to Westward Developments (Totnes) Ltd followed in July 1982, together with Callington bus station to Farm Industries Ltd. Leskinnick garage, Penzance, was also put up for sale, together with depots at Falmouth, Helston, Taunton, Seaton and Minehead and outstations at St Dennis and Dorchester. Numerous offices and other small properties, notably at Camborne, Chard, Kings-bridge and Westward Ho! were also disposed of in the early 1980s. In contrast, detailed drawings for the construction of a bus station and depot at Exmouth had been prepared by NBC's regional architect, and a programme of development was agreed with Devon County Council. The latter was to bear 50% of the cost, and a 99-year lease (!) for occupation of the premises was approved at £40,000. Construction work commenced on 9 July 1979.

In concert with other NBC subsidiaries Western National carried out an extensive programme of 'market analysis' in 1978. After the appropriate

fieldwork was undertaken a Market Analysis Project network designer was appointed on 1 August of that year. Implementation dates of MAP-inspired revisions were as follows:

| Yeovil | 4 February 1980 |
| West Devon | 18 February 1980 |
| East Cornwall | 18 February 1980 |
| West Cornwall | 18 May 1980 |
| West Dorset | 18 May 1980 |
| Torquay | 18 May 1980 |
| North Devon | 7 June 1981 |

The principal outcome was to reduce considerably the number of vehicles employed — and driver/conductors plus engineering staff accordingly.

As elsewhere within the National Bus Company, the turnover of directors and other senior officers at Western National continued apace. Compared, that is, with the stability and progress of the company's

In an attempt to permit its subsidiaries to pick up as many passengers as possible by nipping down side streets, NBC pushed hard for the adoption of what became known as 'midibuses'. Two — a pair of Ford/Alexander 27-seaters — were foisted in 1976 upon Southdown, which promptly passed them on to Western National. Significant, then, that No 3 (LWV 651P) was photographed setting out to collect Paignton schoolchildren in June 1977. *Paul Gainsbury*

A Bristol RELH6G/ECW 45-seater, No 1481 (RDV 432H) was new in 1970 as a coach in Royal Blue livery (albeit with Western National fleetnames), but in 1978, after a spell in National white, it joined a number of its fellows in being altered for one-man-operated stage-carriage service, for which it gained NBC green and white 'local coach' livery. It was photographed four years later in Killigrew Street, Falmouth, operating on the local service around the town and on to Helford Passage. *G. B. Wise*

Western National faithfully preserved the Devon General fleetname. Bristol LH6L/ECW 43-seat saloon No 126 (VDV 106S) was one of seven of its type delivered to WNOC in 1978 in poppy red with Devon General fleetnames. When photographed in April 1982 it was about to depart Okehampton for Exeter, along roads served previously by the by-now-dormant Devon General Omnibus & Touring Co.
*John Marsh*

A latter-day Bristol LHS6L/ECW saloon serving on the old Southern National 25 route (by now Western National's 405) passes through Bridport on its way from West Bay to Burton Bradstock. In addition to being short, these 35-seaters were just 7ft 6in wide, making them ideal for Dorset's narrow country lanes. *A. E. Jones*

early days, when well-known senior officers of long standing had engendered a sense of belonging — a sense which filtered through to all the employees involved in the day-to-day running of a company proud to be part of 'The National'. In contrast, NBC was never 'proper National' in the West Country.

Among the directors, Frank Pointon was replaced by Irwin Dalton; the latter departed within a year, together with G. M. Newberry and R. G. Roberts, who, in turn, were replaced by John Hargreaves and Peter Hunt — more familiarly a 'Chief General Manager' from Central Southern England — who now became 'Divisional Director'. H. W. Taylor joined the ranks soon afterward, only to depart together with Peter Hunt, to be replaced in May 1981 by a returning Irwin Dalton. Robert Brooke and A. P. De Boer had been appointed directors the previous year. G. W. Shaw, Chief Engineer, had departed in 1978 to take up his appointment as General Manager of the Lincolnshire Road Car Co Ltd and was succeeded by J. P. Kennedy. After

some 14 years' tenure Roger Wigmore retired as Secretary in June 1979. His replacement had been but briefly in post when he was appointed General Manager of the Potteries Motor Traction Co Ltd. This game of musical chairs was set to gather momentum as the political pendulum in Britain once again swung to the right.

It is worthy of note that as late as December 1981 the dormant Southern National and Devon General companies were still officially associated creditors of the Western National Omnibus Co Ltd. In that month the directors of both dormant companies agreed that their current accounts with Western National should be regarded as 'long-term loans'. The credit balances thus converted were £900,000 (Southern National) and £1,400,000 (Devon General); also listed in the record is a nominal £1 owed to Greenslades Tours Ltd.

On the vehicle front, the early 1980s saw the purchase (in 1981, from dealer Ensign, of Purfleet, Essex) of 38 Daimler Fleetline double-deckers new to London Transport; these arrived in two batches (13 for £96,826 and 25 for £150,000), some 75 single-deckers going in part-exchange. Maintaining its commitment to National Express coach operation, Western National took delivery of five Dennis Falcon/Duple Goldliner coaches for its (white) Royal Blue fleet in 1982. (See *Glory Days: Royal Blue*.) This was at a time when, following a period when independent F. G. Trathen & Sons of Yelverton had run in competition with National Express, NBC sponsored a corporate venture between that firm and Western National.

The latter had come about as a result of yet another political upheaval which had taken place before the actual implementation of the MAP revisions. Maragaret Thatcher's

In 1981 Western National was one of several NBC subsidiaries to take advantage of London Transport's mass disposal of its DMS-class Daimler Fleetline double-deckers. Reduced to single door, Park Royal-bodied No 816 (TGX 839M) loads at Probus Square *en route* from St Austell to Truro on the morning of 17 August 1985, by which time WNOC had been reduced to a holding company. *A. E. Jones*

Conservative Party had swept to power in 1979; its first radical change for the transport industry had been made in the Transport Act 1980, which had relaxed the regulations relating to long-distance coach operation. More stringent legislation would follow as NBC was obliged to divide its larger subsidiaries into smaller self-contained units, which became in effect a 'pre-privatisation' process.

The proposed reorganisation of Western National as from 1 January 1983 was approved by the NBC board on 7 October 1982. There is nothing in the minutes to suggest that this reorganisation was planned in detail at National House, Exeter. On 4 November 1982 directors Hargreaves, Bodger and Dalton met at Hants & Dorset's headquarters in Bournemouth to discuss the proposed reorganisation and possible amendments to its structure: it would appear that what was originally planned as South Devon Ltd to serve the area around Torbay was the company renamed before its launch as the new Devon General Ltd. A further amendment was that two financially independent units were to be formed within the new Western National Ltd — one for the Cornwall operations and the other for the Plymouth- and Dartmouth-area services. In expressing their appreciation of the help and assistance provided by the General Manager and officers of the Western National Omnibus Co Ltd in the planned reorganisation, the board stressed that the latter 'did not reflect in any way upon the previous administration of the company'. Well, no indeed!

Thus the operational activity of the Western National Omnibus Co Ltd was divided into four limited-liability companies. Meanwhile, each received loans from the former, which now became in effect a holding company *pro tem* in the same way that the old National Omnibus & Transport Co Ltd had functioned all those years before. The four operational companies duly commenced trading with effect from 1 January of 1983, with loans from WNOC as follows:

| | |
|---|---|
| Western National Ltd | £2,500,000 |
| Devon General Ltd | £2,500,000 |
| Southern National Ltd | £1,500,000 |
| North Devon Ltd (trading as Red Bus) | £1,500,000 |

In the words of Michael Rourke, 'the fourth company was North Devon Ltd, which was to serve the old North Devon Area of WNOC. It was thought that it would be an interesting experiment to try to

In July 1982 WNOC gave up its local services in Dorchester — the county town of Dorset, where, 60 years previously, Hants & Dorset had so nearly established a depot. Days before the closure of its outstation near Dorchester South railway station, WNOC's last two locally based vehicles — Bristol LH/ECW No 1629 (VDV 129S) and Leyland National No 2829 (MOD 829P) — were to be found parked in Trinity Street. *A. J. Gwynne*

The early 1980s saw a relaxation of NBC's corporate image. Given increased freedom to be individualistic, Western National experimented with different liveries on vehicles dedicated to certain services. In 1982 Bristol VRT/ECW No 1087 (LOD 727P) was dressed in dark green and white for use on the X35 express service between Portland, Weymouth and Bournemouth. *Martin Curtis*

Whilst Bristol VR No 1087 was at work on the 'Southern Coastlink' express in Dorset, a similar service (X38) was being provided between Exeter and Plymouth as 'Devon's City Link'. Here WNOC No 3537 (FDV 828V), a 49-seat Willowbrook-bodied Leyland Leopard coach of 1979, has arrived at Exeter bus station on the X34 variation. Recalling earlier days on the route, it is parked beside a 'Devon General' Leyland National 2. *G. B. Wise*

operate a very small company on its own as a commercially viable unit; that's why Red Bus came into being. All its allotted buses were, of course, green, so when Bob Montgomery was made Manager of it and decided he'd call his company Red Bus he had a slight problem — all his inherited buses were the wrong colour. So initially he put posters on their sides saying "This is now a Red Bus" — something which got the local press quite excited.'

If the minutes are to be believed, 'Red Bus' seems to have missed out when WNOC approved the transfer of new Timtronic ticket machines with ancillary equipment to Devon General Ltd (at a cost of £433,000), Southern National Ltd (£186,000) and Western National Ltd (£330,000).

Away from the operational side the reorganisation saw the formation of two independent service units — one providing secretarial services, the other in charge of engineering and central stores. The latter, based at WNOC's old central works in Plymouth, became Herald Engineering; from 1983 this represented the only practical 'make and mend' activity undertaken by WNOC, which paid its bills, and whose Chief Engineer was transferred to it as Manager. WNOC Traffic Manager Michael Rourke moved to Taunton to take charge of the new Southern National Ltd.

The Western National Omnibus Co Ltd now concerned itself with such activities as continuing to sell off properties, authorising capital expenditure for building work, providing new equipment for engineering purposes, allocating new vehicles to its subsidiaries, making common arrangements for bank-holiday traffic and, early on, appointing P. R. Wyke-Smith as a director to be concerned solely with the winding-up procedure, which commenced on 1 July 1983. This last proved to be a long-drawn-out process: the board meetings, now held at NBC's headquarters at 172 Buckingham Palace Road, London SW1, lasted until 1987. On 28 February of that year the last 'proper' director of the Western National Omnibus Co Ltd, John Bodger, resigned, to be replaced the following day by the 'winders-up in chief' of the almost-extinct NBC, B. W. French and B. T. Hancock.

The last WNOC directors' meeting was held at 3.15pm on Thursday

14 April 1987. The reports and accounts were perused, and a final Annual General Meeting was announced for 12.30pm on Monday 27 April. That final minute was signed on 9 December 1987. There is nothing on file beyond that date, so that must be considered the last meeting of the Western National Omnibus Co Ltd (Company number 236066). Courtesy of Peter Jaques of the Kithead Trust and the webcheck service provided by Companies House it can be revealed that the last members' list was submitted on 11 May 1987; the last accounts were made up to 31 December 1986, the next accounts due 31 October 1988 (overdue); last returns were made up to 11 May 1987, the next return being due 22 September 1988 (overdue). Yet WNOC had declared itself in members' voluntary liquidation on 15 December 1987. It would appear that the National Bus Company, intending formally to wind up WNOC, for some reason failed to do so.

*Above:* Photographed on 30 August 1984, Leyland Olympian/ECW double-decker No 1810 (A757 VAF) was the property of WNOC's 'subsidiary' Western National Ltd, based at Plymouth with effect from 1 January 1983. Departing that city's Breton Side bus station, the vehicle is decked out in green and white Citybus livery for use on the time-honoured Plymouth Joint Services network. *Adrian A. Thomas*

*Above:* Recorded by a photographer with a sense of history as well as compositional expertise, a late example of the Bristol LHS/ECW combination, No 1560 (FDV 790V), picks up passengers in Market Jew Street, Penzance, on 8 October 1985. By now the property of Western National Ltd, it was bound for the village of Paul, where lies buried Dolly Pentreath of Mousehole, the last fluent speaker of Cornish — and who had a motor bus named after her more than 100 years before this book was published. *Gwyn Griffiths*

*Lower left:* 'Southern National' returns to Weymouth in the form of Michael Rourke's Southern National Ltd. Ex-WNOC 50-seat Leyland National No 2868 (AFJ 707T) coasts into Weymouth along Commercial Road as the Weymouth–Waterloo boat train trundles off for London — a nice reminder of Southern and Western National's railway origins. But, lest we take things too seriously … when informed of the return of 'Southern National' some Weymouth folk replied "well us really didn't notice it had been changed in the first place". *Colin Morris*

*Above:* Symbolising the friendly relationship enjoyed by Veronica Gunn with 'cheek by jowl' operator Hutchings & Cornelius is ex-H&C AEC Reliance/Willowbrook 51-seater FPC 15J, taken over by Safeway two months ahead of the rest of the H&C business. It has just dropped off a passenger in what Latinists call 'Stoke-sub-Hamdon', known to English folk as Stoke-under-Ham (in other words the village beneath Ham Hill, whence since Roman times has come all that beautiful yellow building stone). *Colin Morris*

THE DEMISE of the Western National Omnibus Company brought wry smiles to the faces of several operators in the West Country who, over the years, had enjoyed variable relationships with it in and around the company's established stage-carriage areas. None more so, perhaps, than Veronica Gunn MBE, of South Petherton, Somerset, whose 'Safeway Services' was started by her father and brother in 1928. (See *Southern National Omnibus Company*.) The firm had numerous spats with NO&T's Yeovil and South Petherton-based vehicles. Southern National came next, followed by Western National in 1970, each referred to simply by Veronica as 'The National'. With a winning combination of providing personal service and being a much-loved local personality (indeed, a Somerset lass through and through), book-keeper, conductress and outright owner from 1978, she in that same year purchased the local friendly rival Hutchings & Cornelius Services Ltd — and ultimately outlived 'The National'. Even as the proprietress of the firm she continued to act as a conductress when necessary, and her wit remained as sharp as it was in her comparative youth. I recall boarding a Safeway Bedford OWB in Crewkerne way back in the summer of 1947, during the days when my knowledge of entomology was not too sharp. As she approached to issue my ticket, I noticed with considerable surprise a very large Great Green Grasshopper crawling up the window beside my head. "Good Lord! What is it?" I asked in my 'out-county' tones. "Tiz a Zummerzet vlea," she replied. When I interviewed her at South Petherton in 1982, she said she remembered that; and I believe her.

In one way or another, a ride on a local bus in the West Country was always a colourful experience. National included, of course!

*Left:* She who outlasted 'the National': Miss Veronica Gunn MBE, of Safeway Services, South Petherton, stands proudly before one of her favourite vehicles — a Leyland Leopard — in August 1982. Star of a vigorous televised debate with Transport Minister Barbara Castle, she did not herself own a television set. "What with one thing and another," said she, "I just didn't have time for all that!" How refreshing. *Colin Morris*

*Left:* A familiar sight for following motorists in south Somerset for more than three quarters of a century: the rear of a Safeway Services saloon bus. This one, a Dennis Lancet of 1949, was bodied as a 33-seat coach by Reading of Portsmouth, which builder registered it as ETP 184. Upon restoration it was, for technical reasons, re-registered as ASV 900. *Colin Morris*

A glorious September weekend in 2006 at West Point, Exeter, and a preserved Bristol VRT/ECW — No 1157 (AFJ 764T) —new to Western National in 1979, immaculate in NBC leaf green and white, serves as an overnight windbreak for a marquee pitched by the West Country Historic Omnibus & Transport Trust. Therein, the following day, took place the official book-signing for Ian Allan's *Glory Days: Devon General.* Colin Morris

Readers wishing to learn more about independent operators in the Western National areas or in other parts of the West Country are referred to a series of booklets published by Roger Grimley, details of which can be obtained from:
Old Post, Bigbury, Kingsbridge, Devon, TQ7 4AP.

# Bibliography

Publications found helpful in the compilation of this volume and/or recommended for further reading include:

### Books
Crawley, R. J., MacGregor, D. R., and Simpson, F. D.: *The Years Between — 1909-1969, Vol 1: The National Story to 1929* (D. R. MacGregor, 1979)
Crawley, R. J., and Simpson, F. D.: *The Years Between — 1909-1969, Vol 3: The Story of Western and Southern National from 1929* (Calton Promotions, Exeter, 1990)
Cummings, John: *Railway Motor Buses and Bus Services in the British Isles 1902-1933* Vol 2 (OPC, 1980)
Gentry, P. W.: *Tramways of the West of England* (LRTL, 1952/60)
Hibbs, John: *The History of British Bus Services* (David & Charles, Newton Abbot, 1968)
James, Laurie: *Somerset's Buses* (Tempus, Stroud, 2004)
Kelley, Philip J.: *Road Vehicles of the Great Western Railway* (OPC, 1973)
Klapper, Charles F.: *The Golden Age of Buses* (RKP, 1978)
Morris, Colin: *Hants & Dorset — a history* (DTS Publishing Ltd, Croydon, 1996)
Morris, Colin: *Glory Days: Royal Blue* (Ian Allan, 2000)
Morris, Colin: *Glory Days: Devon General* (Ian Allan, 2006)
Morris, Colin: *Southern National Omnibus Company* (Ian Allan, 2007)
Morris, Colin, and Waller, Andrew: *Wilts & Dorset Motor Services Ltd 1915-1972* (Hobnob Press, Salisbury, 2006)
Rolt, L. T. C.: *Isambard Kingdom Brunel* (Penguin edition, 1990)
Simpson, Frank D.: *The 'Blue Line'* (The Omnibus Society, 1980)
*The Bristol Omnibus Co Ltd* Parts 1 (PH6) and 2 (PH5) (PSV Circle / The Omnibus Society, 1968)
*Western National Omnibus Co Ltd and Southern National Omnibus Co Ltd Part 2 — 1942-79* (PH7) (PSV Circle / The Omnibus Society, 1979)
Whitehouse, Patrick, and St John Thomas, David (editors): *The Great Western Railway — 150 Glorious Years* (Millbrook House, 1985)

### Journals
Numerous articles in *The Engineer, Motor Traction, Motor Transport, Tramway & Railway World, Commercial Motor, Motor Transport Year Book & Directory, Buses Illustrated* and *Buses.*

### Website
WHOTT: www.busmuseum.org.uk